# Write It Right:

Exercises to Unlock the Writer in Everyone

\* \* \*

## Workbook #2

### Unit 4: Point of View (POV)

*By*
**Susan Tuttle**

Susan Tuttle

# Write It Right:
# Exercises to Unlock the Writer In Everyone
# Unit 4: POV

**Copyright 2014 by Susan Tuttle**
**All Rights Reserved**

No part of this book may be reproduced in any form or by mechanical or electronic means including information storage and retrieval systems without permission in writing from the author, except by a reviewer, who may quote brief passages in a review.

Susan's website and blog: www.SusanTuttleWrites.com
Email Susan at: aim2write@yahoo.com
Follow Susan on Twitter: @stuttleauthor, Facebook and LinkedIn

Cover design by: Aaron Kondziela (www.aaronkondziela.com)

A WriterWithin Publication

ISBN-10: 194146503X
ISBN-13: 978-1-941465-03-5

# Write It Right:

## Exercises to Unlock the Writer in Everyone

# Workbook #2:
## Unit 4: Point of View (POV)

# Dedication

One of the greatest attributes a fiction writer can have is a broad view of life, the ability to see events from a multitude of angles. Dad always said, "There are as many ways to see something as there are people to see it." For writers, this ability to see life from more than one perspective is what adds depth and richness to every tale we write.

Therefore, this Workbook Unit II, **Point of View (POV)**, is dedicated to my father, Ed Tuttle, who taught me to have a broad point of view on life. I've never known anyone who enjoyed being alive more than he did, or who had more fun learning something new every day. He could always see everyone's point of view. And he taught me to see the same way.

I miss you more than words can say.

# Contents

**Before You Begin** — i
    Foreword — ii
    Introduction — iv
    The Value of Timed Writing — vii
    Recommended Book List — ix

**Unit #3: Point of View (POV)** — 1
**Section 1: Straight POV**
    Introductionto Straight POV — 5
    Lesson #1: Straight First Person POV — 7
    Lesson #2: Straight Second Person POV — 11
    Lesson #3: Straight Third Person POV — 15

**Section 2: Emotional Omnsicient POV** — 20
    Introduction to Emotional POV — 21
    Lesson #4: Shifting Thirds POV — 24
    Lesson #5: Close Thirds POV — 28
    Lesson #6: Alternating First or Third POV — 33

**Section 3: Classic Omniscient POV** — 38
    Introduction to Classic POV — 39
    Lesson #7: Classic Omniscient POV — 41

**Section 4: Exploring POV** — 46
    Lesson #8: Analysis of POV — 48
    Lesson #9: It's All In The Attitude — 52
    Lesson #10: Clues to Others' Viewpoints — 56

| | |
|---|---|
| Lesson #11: First Person or Third Person? | 63 |
| Lesson #12: Whose Story Is It, Anyway? | 68 |
| Lesson #13: The Unreliable Narrator | 73 |
| Lesson #14: Alternating 1st and 3rd POV | 78 |
| Lesson #15: Correcting POV Inconsistencies | 85 |
| Examples from My Class Writing | 91 |
| **Afterword** | 126 |
| **Susan's Books** | 130 |

# Before You Begin

***SUCCESSFUL STORYTELLING LIES IN*** being able to tell the story you need to tell in the way readers need to hear it. When we do that, we create stories that readers cannot put down. There are many steps along the way. The first three, Character, Setting and Story, are contained in Workbook #1. This volume contains the next most important Unit: ***Point of View (POV)***.

Unlike other books on writing, this volume serves as a workbook to help you hone your writing skills and find your unique voice. Within these pages, you will find **15 exercises** designed **for writers of all levels** that will show you how to identify the correct Point of View for each story you write.

In the few pages that follow is all the front matter that most people simply skip. If you haven't started with Workbook #1, please read what follows, especially the *Foreword* and *The Value of Timed Writing*. They contain invaluable information. If you have read it already, please at least skim *The Value of Timed Writing*, to reacquaint yourself with the "rules" of each lesson.

And of course, don't skip the book list. They are all treasures for your writing library.

# Foreword

**WRITING IS MY LIFE.** I have a thousand stories knocking on the inside of my head, seeking the freedom of paper. I also love to learn, especially about writing and ways to improve my range and skills. But I'm not very disciplined when it comes to how-to books. If it's not a mystery or suspense novel, I lose interest quickly, even if the subject matter is fascinating.

I found that, for me, the best way to learn something is to teach it to someone else. So, three-plus years ago, I decided to start a group where I could teach what I wanted to learn about writing techniques. If nothing else, it would force me to read those "how to write" books I've been collecting.

I formed the *"What If?* Writing Group" through SLO NightWriters on the Central Coast of California. I began with a group of six writers of various writing skills and genres. We met once a week for two hours to explore in depth a specific aspect of fiction writing. I worried at first that, given the weekly commitment, the group would gradually peter out. But not only did they keep showing up, they started arranging appointments and planning trips around the lessons so they wouldn't miss any!

As the year began winding down, I was sure this group would go on its literary way, and I wondered how to attract a new group of students. But when the year was up only one person left the group, due to health problems. Everyone else wanted to repeat the course. We picked up three new members and started again from the beginning, not sure if the original six students would get anything much from the repetition. To the contrary, we discovered the exercises worked just as well as the first time around—and in some instances, even better. It seems that, no matter where you are in your writing journey, or how many times you do these exercises, they continue to work. Every time.

The students are now getting published on a regular basis, and winning awards in writing contests. In fact, three of us won first place awards in different categories at the Central Coast Writers Conference in September of 2011. One even came home with three prizes in the competition! For me, this was proof positive that the **Write It Right** exercises had a hand in unlocking the talent of every member of the group. That's why I added an afternoon class and 8 more students.

The writing successes in both of the *"What If? Writing Groups"* made me wish I could reach more writers with the materials we'd used. But even if I taught classes all day, every day, I could reach only a limited number of writers—and all of them local. I wanted more than that. I wanted to reach all writers, everywhere.

To that end, I decided to collect all the lessons into a series of 12 little instruction booklets (units), a full year-long program called ***Write It Right: Exercises to Unlock the Writer in Everyone.*** This workbook is the second of the series. The first Workbook (Character, Setting, Story) is available in print and digital format from Amazon.com.

# Introduction to Workbook #2

**POINT OF VIEW (POV)** is probably one of the hardest concepts to master, mainly because it has so many subtle nuances. In these pages I define the three major Types of Point of View: straight, emotional and classic. Then I delve into the subdivisions of these POV Types, which brings the types of POV from which you can choose up to seven.

Even well-known, best-selling authors can switch points of view without realizing it, leaving readers scratching their heads in confusion. Readers may not be able to pinpoint exactly what is wrong, that it's a POV switch. But even the most subtle POV deviations can pull them out of the flow of the story and diminish the experience for them. It can leave them feeling that something is somehow off about the story, just a little bit, even if they can't say what it is. And that's not something writers ever want their readers to feel.

The exercises contained in this workbook will help you understand Point of View, choose the correct Point of View for each phase of your story, and begin to recognize those subtle shifts that disturb a reader's concentration and immersion in the tale. As you become more familiar with Point of View, you will begin to recognize those subtle shifts that can occur even in the best of writing.

It won't happen overnight. It takes practice. But the more you work with POV, the better you will become at recognizing even the most obscure problems in your narrative.

It doesn't matter what level you are: beginner, intermediate or advanced. These exercises cross those boundaries and address where you are now in your writing career—and get you to where you want to be.

These are not time-intensive sessions. You only need to **dedicate approximately 30-45 minutes** to each of the fifteen activities, though a few may take longer. Feel free to move at your own pace—one or two exercises a week or a month—but if you choose a fast-track pace, do give yourself enough time assimilate each lesson. It's best to have a couple of days between each exercise. (The *"What If? Writing Group,"* which has used these lessons for over three years as of this writing, does one or two exercises per session, with a week between sessions.)

All you need is a timer and something to write with—pen and paper or computer and keyboard, whichever is most comfortable for you. For maximum results, you might want to pick up a copy of some of the books I've used to formulate these lessons, and which I will reference throughout the course. It's not necessary, though it does make understanding some of the concepts easier.

You can use this volume as a workbook, filling in the pages (though you will need extra paper to finish most of the exercises) as you work through the lessons. But it is best to use separate sheets of paper, or work digitally in a word processing program, so that when you return to the lessons as you feel the need, you won't be distracted by previous answers to the lesson questions.

Always remember, this is **an ongoing process**. Writing is a dynamic art and life is a journey through which you are always growing and learning. Over time your writing will expand and deepen to reflect these life experiences. When you finish this volume (or any of the exercises in the other volumes), you can repeat each of the exercises again, just as we do in "The *What If?* Writing Group"—which at this writing is just beginning its fourth year of repetition with the same students. You'll find that the second, third, and even fourth time around your writing will reach even deeper layers and take you to greater heights. It will be stronger, more compelling and more exciting.

It's a fantastic journey. Plunge into the exercises in **Write It Right: Workbook #2: Point Of View (POV)**, and experience what it means to really understand the narrative potentials available to you.

# The Value of Timed Writing

**MOST OF THE EXERCISES** in this course are timed. You have a specified amount of time to complete each lesson or part of the lesson, usually 15 or 20 minutes. Thirty at the most. That's it. Period.

Why timed writing? There are two major benefits to timed-limited sessions. As **Natalie Goldman** shows in **Writing Down The Bones**, timed writing exercises force you to keep writing. You have a specific goal and only a short time in which to accomplish it. You have to step out of your way, turn off your inner editor—who is constantly telling you you've used the wrong word, no one will believe that plot, your characters aren't "real" enough, etc.—and simply write. From your heart, from your subconscious instincts, from the place where your stories live. It's authentic writing that's scraped to the bone of emotion. It's compelling and readers will want more.

The second benefit is that you learn to trust yourself and your writing process. When we learn to put our conscious mind on hold and just let the words flow, amazing things happen. Stories emerge that we never knew were there. Connections get made that our conscious minds would never have considered. Best of all, our authentic voice emerges, announcing in clear, ringing tones, "This is who I am as a writer. This is what I need to say." Timed writing exercises will introduce you to yourself.

Timed exercises allow you to step away from your editor self and into your writer self because you don't have time to think. You have to just keep writing, no matter what comes out. It may be hard at first not to go back and correct that word, rethink that action, direct the flow, etc. It takes time to learn to trust your instincts. When you find yourself wanting to go back, don't. *Write* about wanting to go back until you return to the natural flow of the exercise. You can always cut out the extraneous parts later. That's what editing is for.

## *Timed Writing Format "Rules"*

Read the lesson, make sure you understand what to do, then set your timer and write until it dings. Don't stop to think, don't edit as you go, just keep your pen moving or your fingers typing on the keyboard. If you can't think of anything at first, write about not being able to think of anything and just see what happens. Repeat for the next lesson. And the next, and the next...

Also, be aware that my use of the terms "character," "person," "people," "he" and "she" are meant to indicate the protagonists, antagonists and other characters in your stories, whether they be humans, animals or otherworldly creatures. Make whatever adjustments you need to make to each exercise, so that it fits your specific genre and character choice.

**Note:** An asterisk at the end of an exercise denotes that there is an example of that exercise from my own writing at the end of the section.

# Recommended Book List

**THESE BOOKS, AMONG OTHERS**, have been instrumental in the formation of these lessons. Throughout the course I will reference the pertinent page or pages to read in the appropriate volume. Although you don't need these books to complete the lessons, the information they contain is invaluable. It will add to your knowledge and skills and enhance your learning throughout this series. And they will form a solid foundation for your writer's reference library.

I am listing the copyright year for each volume, so that if you want to read the suggested pages, you will have the correct volume in which to find them. How-to books are often updated with new examples and insights. If you obtain a volume published after the dates listed below, you will still get the same fantastic writing information. But because things will have shifted around in newer editions, you might have trouble finding the proper references for each lesson unless you use a volume with the same publication date as those listed below.

> *Write Away* by Elizabeth George (2004)
> *What If? Writing Exercise for Writers* by Anne Bernays and Pamela Painter (1990)
> *On Writing* by Stephen King (2000)
> *Characters & Viewpoint* by Orson Scott Card (1988)
> *How to Write a Damn Good Novel* by James N. Frey (1987)
> *The Novel Writer's Toolkit* by Bob Mayer (2003)
> *Finding Your Writer's Voice: A Guide to Creative Fiction* by Thaisa Frank and Dorothy Wall (1994)
> *The 38 Most Common Fiction Writing Mistakes* by Jack M. Bickham (1992)

And every writer's library should contain the following reference volumes:
> ***The biggest dictionary** you can afford (check used bookstores for bargains). There's no substitute for a good, print dictionary
> **Roget's Thesaurus*
> **Sisson's Synonms* (if you can find it)
> **The Elements of Style* (Strunk and White)
> **Barron's Essentials of English*

# Unit #4: Point of View (POV)

*"We begin to learn wisely when we're willing to see world from other people's perspectives."*

~Toba Beta, *Master of Stupidity*

**REMEMBER THE STORY ABOUT** the three blind men describing an elephant? One thought it was like a pillar (leg), one a huge snake (trunk), one a sinewy vine (tail). Each one had a different view of what the animal looked like, depending on which part of the body they were touching. Their Point of View (POV) depended on their experience.

For fiction writers, **POV is a critical issue**. Choosing the correct POV for each of our stories has a huge impact on the success of the story itself. The wrong POV can make a story crash and burn. The right POV can lift the story from ordinary to extraordinary. Depending on which POV we use, our story can change as drastically in form, plot and direction as the descriptions of the elephant from blind man to blind man.

POV is a slippery concept for most writers. We understand intellectually what it means to write from a particular person's point of view: We can only write what that person experiences, knows, thinks and feels. Nothing else.

And yet, our stories are made up of a multitude of characters, scenes and events, all of which dovetail into each other in some way. Sometimes it's important for the reader to know what Character A is thinking, and it's equally important for them to know what Character B is feeling. And at the same time, they need to know what Character C is doing.

If this were a hundred years ago, we wouldn't have as much emphasis on Point of View. Most stories were written from what is today referred to as an Omniscient POV, meaning authors jumped in and out of all the characters' heads willy-nilly, and even inserted their own observations into the narrative. Audiences back then didn't mind that.

But as novel writing grew more sophisticated, and various genres made their debuts, more rules came into use to help keep things straight for not only readers but also for writers. Then media such as radio, movies and television further eroded the freedom writers had to dip into their characters' heads any way they wanted to, by showing stories from only one or two characters' points of view.

Audiences, and hence readers, became used to concentrating on, and connecting with, one particular character at a time. Jumping from head to head kept them from making that connection. It broke their concentration. And the concept of POV Types solidified. That made things easier—and harder—for the writer.

So, in effect, not counting the variations, today we have (all of which will be explained thoroughly in Lessons #1—#7):

**A. Straight POV Types**
    Straight First Person

    Straight Second Person
    Straight Third Person
**B. Emotional Omniscient POV Types**
    Shifting Third Person
    Close Third Person
    Alternating First or Third Person
**C. Classic Omniscient Third Person**

Only by thoroughly understanding the various types of POV that are available for us to choose from can we know which type is best for the story we are writing. Knowing the right POV for each story can even help us decide whose story it is, and which character's POV tells it best. Sometimes the right POV even changes whose story it is.

**Section 1** details the various types of Straight Points of View (POVs) that have evolved. **Section 2** discusses the Emotional Omniscient Points of View. **In Section 3** you will work in Classic Omniscient POV. There are advantages and disadvantages for each. Knowing the limitations of each one will help you not only choose the correct one for your stories, but also stay within the bounds of your chosen POV's limitations.

For all the exercises in Parts 1, 2 and 3, you will be working with **the same scene**. Make it a scene between two people, with a good mix of narrative and dialogue. Be sure to include some obvious conflict. The easiest way to do this is to use a situation that has conflict built into it. By this I mean such scenes as a car accident, a purse snatching, an argument between two people in a crowded public place, an occupied building on fire, etc. These types of situations have intrigue and high suspense as an integral ingredient. Having a high amount of tension built into the situation will keep you from getting bored with the rewrites you will be doing throughout Parts I and II.

You can, of course, use a scene from a story you are working on, as long as it has enough inherent suspense or tension to hold your interest through the various rewrites.

In **Section 4** we will explore variations on the standard POVs, with exercises on how to give clues to other characters' POVs, characters' attitudes and using an unreliable narrator. You will also gain experience in recognizing various inconsistencies in POV in a variety of different passages.

The fifth part of this workbook contains examples of what I wrote while doing these exercises. These pieces were done during my *What If? Writing Group* classes right along with my students. They are as produced, without any further editing or correction of syntax, spelling/typos or punctuation. An asterisk after the Exercise Title marks which lessons have corresponding examples from my writing work.

# Introduction to Straight POV

**STRAIGHT POINT OF VIEW** (POV): A story written from one person's point of view. We understand intellectually that it means we pick one character and then only write what that person experiences, knows, thinks and feels. Nothing else. Simple, right?

Sure, if we only had one character in the story. But our stories are made up of many characters, or we wouldn't have a story. And what if we have a critical scene and our POV character isn't in it? Or what if Character A is our POV Character, but what Character B is thinking or feeling is absolutely critical to the reader's understanding of the story?

These are all valid considerations when deciding to write in a Straight Point of View. But even if we solve all these potential problems and keep the story in one character's POV, we still have another hurdle to face. We have to know the character well enough so that his/her voice is unique and consistent throughout the entire narrative. This is not as easy as you might think, especially in a novel-length work. (For more on creating characters, see the lessons in Unit #1 in the *Write It Right Workbook #1*)

There are three Straight POVs: First person straight, second person straight and third person straight. In other words, you would be writing

I/we, you, or he/she/they. Each Straight POV has its own unique benefits and drawbacks. Knowing the parameters of each one, and having experience in writing it, will help you decide which one, if any, is right for the particular story you want to tell.

**READ:** *The Novel Writer's Toolkit* (Mayer, 2003) Page 107, starting with Point of View and ending on page 109 before First Person Point of View.

# Lesson #1: Straight First Person POV

**STRAIGHT FIRST PERSON POINT** of View (POV) uses a single character narrating the tale in the first person, that is, in "I" and "we" format. It makes the story feel like a diary entry, or a letter written to someone. Or perhaps the "I" character is telling what happened to a friend or relative. It is this character's personal story.

Straight First Person is the easiest of the POV forms to understand because the "I" format makes it obvious that you can only tell what the "I" character in the story knows and experiences herself. Things that happen to other people—off stage, as it were—are out of bounds. The only way the narrating character, the "I" of the story, can tell any of that is if someone else tells him first. For this reason, many (though not all) First Person POV stories feature the protagonist as the "I" character.

Another great advantage to First Person POV is that there is very little distance between the reader and the narrator. It has quite a personal feel, as though the reader is sitting with the narrator in a confidential setting, listening to the intimate details of his/her life story. It can make for very compelling reading.

One main disadvantage to using First Person POV is that it is one of the most difficult to write well, because its success hinges on **total consistency of the voice**. Every word must be filtered through one person and one person only, with all his prejudices, biases, education (or lack thereof), quirks, speech patterns, unique view of the world, etc. The writer must, in a very real sense, become the narrating character or the POV will not hold together.

There are other limitations to using Straight First Person POV, the biggest of which is not knowing what happens when the "I" is not there to see or hear it. That means the narrating character must be onstage for the entire book, or devices such as phone calls, letters, news articles and expository scenes between the "I" and other characters must be used to give necessary information to both the "I" narrator and the reader. This can lead to unrealistic, obviously contrived or overly convoluted plots. And if major events take place off stage, it lessens the tension needed to keep readers turning pages.

Another drawback is that the "I" narrator cannot know what other characters are thinking, feeling or planning unless they tell her. She can only guess. Depending on how this is handled, it can either hurt or enhance the story.

You, the writer, are completely absent in this mode. **Nothing can be revealed until the "I" character learns of it**. Also, time and tense can become an issue. Is the narrator remembering what happened in the past, or is it happening as she relates it, in the present? If there is no distance in time between events and narration, will the "I" character's strong emotions prevent him from telling his story coherently? Will he get lost in the depth of his feelings and lose the thread of the story? Will the intimacy between readers and character be too close for readers to handle all those very strong emotions? These are all important points to consider when considering First Person POV to tell your story.

Straight First Person POV is also the only POV form in which the narrator and the POV character are the same. In all other POVs, there is a narrator who is telling the story as if it were the POV character. In Straight First Person POV the narrator does not become the POV character, the narrator actually is the POV character.

Straight First Person POV can be written equally effectively in either past or present tense.

**READ:** *The Novel Writer's Toolkit* (Mayer, 2003) Page 109, "First Person Point of View," ending on Page 111 after #2.

# Exercise #1: Straight First Person*

(Purpose of Exercise: To Explore Straight First Person POV)

**CREATE A SCENE BETWEEN** two people, making it an action scene of some kind that is a good balance between dialogue, inner thought and narration. Be sure you have some inherent tension in the scene. Choose a scene from a piece on which you are working, or use one of the following scenarios, setting it in a public place. This is the scene you will be using for the next 6 exercises, so make it one that truly excites you:

    A car accident

    A purse snatching

    An argument between two people

A fire in an occupied building

A date gone wrong

A rivalry between two sports figures

The aftermath of revealing a dangerous or devastating secret

A controversy at an awards ceremony

Write your chosen scene in **First Person POV**. Choose one of the characters (Character A or Character B) to use as the POV character; i.e., the "I" of the story, the one who is telling what happened. Remember that you can only tell what the "I" character knows, feels, thinks, sees, hears and experiences. And you must know who your character is, what prejudices, biases, speech patterns, etc., he or she has and make sure to stay consistent throughout the scene.

Set your timer for **20 MINUTES** and start writing.

When you have finished, read your scene and check to make sure there is nothing there that the "I" character could not know, see, hear, feel (both physically and emotionally), smell, say or think.

# Lesson #2: Straight Second Person POV

**STRAIGHT SECOND PERSON POINT** of View (POV) uses "you" in place of "I" or "he/she." The narrating character is unseen and unknown as the story is defined for the reader. This point of view **puts the reader into the central character's place.** In effect, it makes the reader become the main character, the person who is actually undergoing the narrated events.

Straight Second Person POV is rarely used in fiction. It most often feels awkward in both the writing and the reading and creates a vast distance between a fiction story and the reader. In fiction, readers of Straight Second Person POV stories may feel either preached at or ordered around, and they rarely forget they are reading fiction.

The major problem with Straight Second Person POV is that it is very hard to create the necessary sympathetic bond between the reader and the main character, **when the main character is the reader**. The bond between reader and character is what keeps readers reading. Without it, readers won't care enough about the protagonist to continue on. They won't care what happens to him. The writer runs the very real risk that the protagonist of a "you" story is vastly different from the reader in outlook and personality, and in the decisions she makes and in what she does. In that case, there will be no connection between reader and character at all. The reader will spend the entire time questioning and arguing about the actions that "she" is doing, because she, the reader, wouldn't do that. It takes an amazing amount of skill to convince the reader that she **actually is** the character, and not just pretending to be the character. Doubly so when the reader is the opposite sex of the main character.

That is why Straight Second Person POV is rarely used in novels and not much more often in short stories. It is used most successfully in nonfiction books like this one. In nonfiction, no one is trying to hide the fact that there is an author who is writing and imparting ideas. That does not work in fiction. The fiction author always needs to be an unseen puppet-master, the person hidden behind the curtain who keeps the illusion going through invisible magic.

A skilled writer can, depending on the story, overcome these drawbacks to create a compelling Straight Second Person POV tale. It's a matter of choosing the just right story and the right situation, and working to create a bond that will entice readers to continue. Straight Second Person POV works equally well in either present or past tense, depending on the story.

**READ:** *The Novel Writer's Toolkit* (Mayer, 2003) Page 111, "About Second Point of View"

# Exercise #2: POV Types—Straight Second Person*

(Purpose of Exercise: To Explore Straight Second Person POV)

**REWRITE THE SCENE YOU** created in Exercise #1, using the same character you chose as your POV character in Exercise #1, this time writing in Second Person POV. You, the writer-as-narrator, are now telling the "I" character what to do and how he or she feels, using "you" to do so.

For example, in Exercise #1 you may have written a sentence like this:

"I walked into the room on shaky legs, certain that everyone knew what I had done and were hoping to see me stumble and fall."

In Second Person POV, it might read something like:

"You walked into the room. Your legs felt shaky. You were sure that everyone was waiting for you to stumble and fall, because you were certain that they knew what you had done."

Think carefully about what needs to change to make your scene a success in Second Person POV. Can the events stay exactly the same, or do they need to be adjusted to fit the viewpoint? Can the character remain the same, personality-wise? Can things happen in the same sequence, and for the same reasons?

You might find this scene translates well into Second Person, or that Second Person is not a viable option. Even though you may never write a Second Person POV story, exploring this POV type through this exercise will help you understand its advantages and disadvantages, so if that perfect Second Person POV story does come along, you will be able to recognize it.

Now re-read your First Person POV scene, then give yourself **15 MINUTES** to rewrite it in Second Person POV.

# Lesson #3: Straight Third Person POV

**STRAIGHT THIRD PERSON POINT** of View (POV) is the most familiar and most often used POV. It is what most readers are comfortable with, if for no other reason than vast exposure to the format. Most novels for the last hundred years or so that have not used Straight First Person POV have been written in Third Person POV, either Straight or Emotional Omniscient. It is the most prevalent of the POV types in use today.

In Straight Third Person POV, there is a narrator who is telling the story (not the writer), through the eyes of one of the main characters. It can be the protagonist, the antagonist, or even one of the sidekicks. (In the Sherlock Holmes stories, Conan Doyle used Holmes' sidekick, Watson, as the POV character instead of Holmes himself.) So, in essence, you have the writer, then the narrator who tells the story, then the POV character through whose eyes the story is sifted.

This format uses "he" and "she" and "they." It can be written in past tense (He walked down the road.) or in present tense (He walks down the road.), though past tense is most often used and is the one readers are most comfortable with. Many readers find present tense in Third Person POV to be rather disconcerting because it can feel too immediate. It takes a skilled hand to make present tense compelling to readers. Keep this in mind when choosing not only the POV type for your story, but also whether you want it in past or present tense.

Straight Third Person POV format creates less distance between reader and characters than Straight Second Person POV, but more than Straight First Person POV. It's a comfortable in-between place for readers. As readers become more and more immersed in the story, and more vested in the outcome for the characters, this distance begins to vanish. It's as though the reader were sitting on the POV character's shoulder, or perhaps slipping into his or her body like a second spirit, to relive the events **with** the character. And because of the distance maintained in Third Person, especially in past tense, readers can more easily handle strong emotions.

Skilled writers can create a microcosm so compelling that when the reader steps into this world, the outer—or real—world vanishes. We've all read books that have pulled us so deeply into the story that we no longer heard the sounds around us, were no longer aware that we were sitting in a chair holding a book in our hands. That is our goal as storytellers: To create a world so real nothing else exists for the duration of the reading.

The biggest advantage of Straight Third Person POV is that we can delve as deeply as we need to into our POV character's psyche. We can create an almost unbreakable bond between readers and the POV character. By the time the story is finished, readers will feel they know that character as well as, or perhaps even more than, they know their own friends and family members. They will ache for her, cry for her, root for her, suffer with her. And feel the same satisfaction at her success—and the same pain at her failure—as she does.

This is a great advantage for the writer, because this intense bond with the POV character is what keeps readers turning pages. The major drawback of Straight Third Person POV is the same as with Straight First Person POV: the narrator is limited to the POV character's view and cannot tell the reader anything that happens outside the POV character's milieu. This means the POV character needs to be "on stage" for a lot of the action, or must be alerted to facts by other characters and devices.

However, this POV type has **a bit more latitude in voice** than First Person, since there is a narrator who is telling the story. This is not just a change in pronoun, from "I" to "he" or "she." Unlike Straight First Person POV, where the character is the one actually telling the story, here the **narrator is telling the story as if it were the character**. Therefore, some of the narrator's voice will blend with the voice of the POV character.

To make this concept clearer, imagine the difference between your mother telling a story about something she did, and you telling the same story about her as if you were her. Her story will be purely her; her own voice, her own words, her own gestures. Though you may do your best to imitate her, little pieces of your own voice and mannerisms will "bleed" through, simply because you are not her. You are only pretending to be. You are a narrator telling a story, not the person the events happened to.

The writer is still absent in this POV format. **The narrator's voice is not the writer's voice.** It is the pseudo-voice of someone pretending to be the POV character.

There are ways around the limitations of Straight Third Person POV. It's called Emotional Omniscience, which we will explore in the next three lessons. There are distinct advantages and disadvantages to each of those POV types, just like there are for the Straight POV types, and understanding all of them will help you choose the right Third Person POV (Straight or Emotional Omniscient) for each of your stories.

**READ:** *The Novel Writer's Toolkit* (Mayer, 2003) Page 112, Third Person Point of View to Page 113, ending just before Third Person Shifting (we will cover that sub-type of POV in a later lesson).

# Exercise #3: POV Types—Straight Third Person*

(Purpose of Lesson: To Explore Straight Third Person POV)

**REWRITE YOUR ORIGINAL SCENE** again, this time using Third Person (ie, he or she) for the POV character. Use the same POV character you used for the first two exercises and make whatever changes are necessary to the scene so it fits this viewpoint.

Again, this is not simply a matter of changing all the "I's" to "he" or "she." Consider carefully as you write if any actions need to be changed or adjusted, or if the character's perceptions need to be expressed differently now that there is a narrator relating the story (filtered through the POV character's eyes and mind, of course). You may find more opportunity to express deep-set emotions and motivations that had not come out in First Person POV. That little bit of distance between reader and character, and the little bit of difference between the narrator being the POV character and only pretending to be, can make a big difference in the narrative.

Just make sure you stick with the same POV character you have been working with, and remember that you cannot put in anything that he or she does not feel, see, experience, hear or do him- or herself. When you finish, reread your scene and check for any POV inconsistencies.

Set the timer for **15 MINUTES** and begin.

# Emotional Omniscient POV

**WHY DO I CALL** these types of POV **emotional**? Because that is the base of these types: the emotions of the characters. This is not a distinction that is made in the general literature on Omniscient POV. But for me, to be able to understand the differences in the various POV types, I needed to be more specific in naming them.

The main difference between Straight and Omniscient POV types comes from their titles: Straight denotes that only one character serves as the Point of View Character. Omniscient POV allows the writer to use more than one character as the Point of View Character. It may sound simple in theory, but it practice this distinction has caused many a writer to pull out wads of hair. Me included.

The value of using an Emotional Omniscient POV is that it gives readers a deeper understanding of the main characters. And that, when done well, compels the reader to turn pages, and to look for more books by the same author. A win-win, yes?

# Introduction to Emotional Omniscient POV

**THE USE OF OMNISCIENCE,** when applied to Point of View, allows the writer greater latitude in storytelling because it allows us to access the thoughts and feelings of more than one character in a story. In this section we will be exploring what I call **Emotional Omniscience**.

Omniscient means "all seeing," and applied to literature it means the narrator is able to "see" more. The narrator can switch from one POV character to another to tell the story.

There are three ways this switch can be accomplished:
1. **Shifting**
2. **Close**
3. **Alternating**

Most Emotional Omniscient POVs are used with Third Person. This is because switching POV in either First or Second Person presents almost insurmountable problems in identifying the POV characters properly to avoid confusing readers. The only viable option for Emotional Omniscience in First Person POV is Alternating. Therefore, the first two types of Emotional Omniscient POV in this section will concentrate on Third Person Emotional Omniscient POV. Only the last one, Alternating, will refer to First Person narrative thread also.

Therefore, in talking about modern Emotional Omniscience in literature, we have:

**Shifting Third Person POV** (Shifting Thirds)

**Close Third Person POV** (Close Thirds)

**Alternating Third Person POV** (Alternating Firsts and/or Thirds)

The advent of first radio plays, then movies, television and videos has changed the way we write. As stated before, a hundred or so years in the past, point of view was mostly done as Shifting Thirds, where the author dipped into and out of all the characters' heads whenever he wanted to—even within the same paragraph.

Author intrusion—i.e., the author inserting his/her own thoughts, feelings or conclusions into the action of the story—was also a common practice. Authors often "spoke" directly to their reading audiences, using such devices as, "dear reader" and parenthetical "you" expressions. [For example: He told her he loved her and she believed him. (You, dear reader, know him for a liar.) The poor thing began planning their wedding from that day forward.]

Once audio and video audiences began to be more familiar and comfortable with stories told from one character's point of view, printed stories followed suit. The use of Shifting Emotional Omniscient POV declined (though it is still prevalent in the romance, romantic suspense, sci-fi and fantasy genres—without author intrusion, of course), and stories concentrated on narration using only one character: Straight First or Third Person POV. Then emotional omniscient variations came into use, each with their own rules to follow: Close Thirds and Alternating Firsts and/or Thirds.

Classic Omniscient POV is in a category by itself because it is **not emotional**. It does not allow the writer to enter into any of the characters' heads. Exercise #7 will acquaint you with this form of POV. It is included in this section because it is an Omniscient POV, though of a form less rarely used today.

The following three exercises in emotional omniscient POV, as well as the one in the following section on Classic Omniscient POV, will help acquaint you with four types of omniscience, so that you can choose the right POV for your stories.

# Lesson #4: Emotional Omniscient Shifting Thirds

**I HAVE MY OWN DEFINITION** of Omniscience in writing, because there doesn't seem to be agreement on what to call having more than one POV character in a story, other than the generic term Omniscience. Some define an Omniscient POV as being able to enter into any character's mind at any time. Others say Omniscient POV means the narrator does not enter anyone's mind at any time, but simply tells what happens in the story. Others define it as somewhere in between these two.

I call being able to access any character's thoughts at any time **Shifting Thirds**. I think the word Shifting best expresses the concept—the ability to move (shift) back and forth among minds at will. This is the POV used in many classic novels, especially those written in the Nineteenth and first half of the Twentieth Centuries. Though mostly frowned upon today in the vast majority of novels, Shifting Thirds is still prevalent in such genres as romance, science fiction and fantasy.

This POV type is very attractive to the less experienced novelist, because it lets the writer indulge in the exploration of what everyone is thinking and feeling. As writers, we think every minute detail of our story carries the same importance. It is only through experience that we learn that the vast majority of what we want to put into our book doesn't really belong there. It's either unnecessary backstory or irrelevant detail. Everything has to work toward moving the story forward. If it doesn't, it needs to be cut.

The danger in Shifting Thirds POV lies in the temptation to use it to enlighten the reader to even incidental characters' thoughts and feelings, regardless of whether they advance the story. I was guilty of that in the first few books I wrote, dipping into even minor characters' heads. In one story I even expounded on the thoughts of a messenger who appeared only once simply to hand the main protagonist a letter. Needless to say, these novels still sit in a drawer, awaiting major overhaul.

It also takes a great deal of skill to shift seamlessly from one mind to another, sometimes even within the same paragraph. If this is not done with superb finesse, it can at best feel choppy, and at worst confuse readers about who is feeling and thinking what. And once readers get confused about which character they are reading about, once they have to stop and go back to figure it out, they usually lose interest and put the book down. After all, reading novels should be fun, not work.

All this shifting around can also create distance between the reader and the characters, because we are never in any one character's head long enough to truly bond. It's harder for readers to empathize, to care, to want to know what will happen to the characters because they don't know them that well, and therefore they may stop turning those pages.

However, done with skill and finesse, Shifting Thirds POV can actually enhance the reading experience, because it lets readers viscerally feel everything **all** the main characters are feeling, not just one of them. Done right, it can create a very intense connection to the characters that compels readers to finish the story. (For an example of a true master at Shifting Thirds POV, pick up a romance book by Nora Roberts. And if romance isn't your cup of tea, try one of her futuristic police procedural mysteries written under the name J.D. Robb. Her seamless shifting into and out of her main character's heads is well worth studying.)

**READ:** *Character And Viewpoint* (Card) Page 155 - 157, ending at "Changing Viewpoint Characters."

## *Exercise #4: Emotional Omniscient POV Types—Shifting Thirds**

(Purpose of Exercise: To Explore Shifting Thirds POV)

***FOR THIS REWRITE OF*** your scene, employ Shifting Thirds POV. You can let the reader know what is going on inside the heads of both characters in the scene, switching from one to the next whenever you feel like it.

For example, you might write something like this:

> Kelly walked into the room on shaky legs, certain that everyone knew what she had done and were hoping to see her stumble and fall. But she had her pride. She'd be damned if she let these old biddies keep her from accepting this award. She lifted her chin and fixed her gaze on the podium as she moved forward.

Janet watched Kelly stalk across the room and felt the breath catch in her throat. She couldn't believe that witch had the nerve to show up. She wanted to intercept her, beat her to a pulp in front of everyone. Janet's hands curled into fists as she fought for control. She looked at Brad, who winked at her, well aware of the emotions roiling inside her. He wondered what she would say if she knew he'd spent last night with Kelly. In her condo. In her bed. He doubted he'd get lucky tonight if Janet found out about that.

Within these two paragraphs, we have been inside three heads: that of Kelly, Janet and even Brad.

Now take your original scene and shift in and out of your two characters' heads as you rewrite it. Consider what needs to change, what new information might come into view, how relationships—or even the story itself— might change using this POV type.

Give yourself **15 MINUTES** for this rewrite.

# Lesson #5: Emotional Omniscient POV—Close Thirds

**CLOSE THIRDS POV MEANS** that writers can switch from one character's head into another's to tell the story, but not as often as in Shifting Thirds. An entire scene—and usually more—will be rendered from one character's point of view before switching to another character. One character may even carry a good portion of a chapter before another character picks up the story line. Sometimes a full chapter, or even two or three, will be narrated from Character A's point of view, and the next two or three chapters from Character B's point of view.

Using Close Thirds for your POV format allows your readers to quickly build strong connections with more than one character in the story because they get to spend an extended amount of time with each of them. They get to understand how two, three or more characters are impacted by events, and they can bond with the one or two who most appeal to them. The entire burden of connection is not vested in just one character. This often gives the story a wider audience appeal.

The main drawback when using Close Thirds is that if switching POVs is not done with smooth transitions and skill, readers **may not realize there has been a switch**. They will lose sight of which character is now telling the story and will become bewildered while reading. Also, the flow of the story can feel choppy if the POV is switched too often or too closely together. That, too, confuses readers, who then will have a tendency to put the book or story down.

Another drawback is having too many POV characters in the story. Make sure you choose only those whose interior thoughts, feelings and motivations are most important to **moving the story forward.** This is a prime example of when "less is more." For example, if you have two co-protagonists and one antagonist, you might choose to write the story back and forth among these three characters. But you wouldn't necessarily use the protagonist's two sidekicks or the antagonist's four helpers to also tell part of the story, because too many POV characters can confuse the reader. Unless, of course, what **one** of those sidekicks or helpers thinks, his/her motivation, is crucial to the story and there's no other seamless way to get the information in.

There are three important things to remember when writing in Close Thirds POV.

***First**, it is imperative to decide **what portion of the story belongs to which character**. In other words, who is the best character to tell what happens in this part of the story? It might be the protagonist, or perhaps a secondary character. Or even the antagonist.

***Second**, keep in mind that **each POV character's voice must be consistent** throughout that character's portion of the story. For the duration of that character's POV narration, Straight POV rules apply. Nothing can be related that the POV character does not know, see, feel, hear, think, etc. The narrator must mimic the POV character every bit as effectively as it does in a Straight Third Person POV story, or the illusion will fall apart. It's also important to make sure that each POV character's voice is **noticeably different.** If all the POV characters sound alike, that, too, will generate confusion in the reader.

***Third**, it's crucial that the writer give the reader **a clear indication that there is a switch in POV** character. If this isn't done, readers will not know when the switch occurs. They will not be able to tell who is now narrating the story and often will lose the thread of the story itself. That leads to putting the book down. It also leads to not trusting this particular author to tell a story worth taking the time to read, and that reader will probably never read anything by that author again.

So, in a nutshell:
1. Know which character this part of the story belongs to
2. Keep the POV character's voice consistent in each part
3. Indicate clearly there is a POV switch

Close Thirds POV is most effective when a chapter is divided 2/3 for one character and 1/3 for another, although there are many other effective ways to split the story among the main characters.

The secret of success is in **choosing the correct POV Character for each portion,** whether it's half a chapter, a full chapter or more than one chapter. Always ask yourself: whose story is this part of the chapter? Who can best tell what happens here? Sometimes the answer is not the character you first thought it would be.

How do we give a clear signal to the reader that there is a POV switch? Again, there are **three techniques** to keep in mind, **all** of which should be used for **every** POV switch:

1) Make each POV character's voice **different and unique.**

2) Identify the POV character **by name** within the first two sentences of his/her section.

3) Insert a **"line break"** (an extra two blank lines of space between paragraphs) whenever you switch to a new POV character. (A line break is also used to show a large gap in time, or a change of setting, which is why it's necessary to also identify the character within the first two sentences.)

# Exercise #5: Emotional Omniscient POV Types—Close Thirds*

(Purpose of Exercise: To Explore Close Thirds POV)

**REWRITE YOUR ORIGINAL SCENE** from Exercise #1, this time changing from Character A to Character B after you have written a large portion of the scene from the first character's POV. You might write the bulk of the scene from Character A's POV, then switch to Character B (after a line break) to finish the scene, or let Character A finish the entire scene and then, after the line break, let Character B tell what happens after it ends.

Be sure to keep in mind that when you are in Character A's head, you can only write what that character sees, hears, does, feels, etc. Make sure you stay true to that character's voice all the way through his/her portion of the scene. Be consistent with the character's voice until you switch.

When you have completed Character A's portion of the scene, skip two lines for a line break and begin writing from Character B's POV. Try to make this character's voice distinct from the first, which includes his/her manner of speaking, word choices, outlook on life, personality, etc. And don't forget to identify this character in the first two sentences.

When you finish this rewrite, read it to make sure you have stayed in the appropriate character's point of view in each section. Make any changes you may need to make.

Give yourself **25 MINUTES** for this exercise, starting now.

# Lesson #6: Emotional Omniscient POV Types—Alternating POV

**THE LAST EMOTIONAL OMNISCIENT POV** form that allows the writer to explore thought and emotion is one I call **Alternating POV**. In this form of Emotional Omniscient POV, the story alternates among two, three or four characters, **chapter by chapter or section by section**. Alternating POVs can be written in either First or Third Person format.

This is how Alternating POV works. Each chapter of the book is dedicated to a specific character, who tells that portion of the story through the narrator. Each chapter heading usually indicates who the POV Character is by stating the Character's name immediately beneath the chapter head or title. The POV character must **also be identified in the first few lines** of the chapter because—shocking as it is for us writers who consider our every word to be golden—most readers **do not read** the chapter headings.

With two POV Characters, chapters might look like this:

Chapter 1: Character A's POV

Chapter 2: Character B's POV
Chapter 3: Character A's POV
Chapter 4: Character B's POV

And if we have three Alternating POV Characters, we might have chapters structured this way:

Chapter 1: Character A's POV
Chapter 2: Character B's POV
Chapter 3: Character C's POV
Chapter 4: Character A's POV
Chapter 5: Character C's POV
Chapter 6: Character B's POV

This can be a fun way to write a story that hinges on misinformation and misunderstandings among the characters. Each main character in the story gets to detail his or her view of what is happening, complete with wrong decisions based on faulty facts. It is also an effective type to use when telling the story of individuals who do not meet until later in the book, but whose individual stories lead them inexorably to that meeting.

Alternating POVs can also allow writers to go back to the beginning of the story, or of a scene or an event, and tell it from the different characters' perspectives. In an Alternating POV story, all the POV characters have equal weight and impact on events and the outcomes **in their portion of the story**.

Alternating POV succeeds only if **each POV voice is distinct and clearly recognizable** to readers, **especially** if the story is written in First Person format. Readers must be able to distinguish from the first couple of sentences that the POV has switched to a new character, regardless of any identifying information stated in the Chapter header. It is imperative that the POV character be identified in the first few sentences of each chapter. Do not fall into the trap of assuming readers will note the name under the chapter heading. Some will, but many won't, especially if the chapter headers are generic (Chapter One—Andrew; Chapter Two—Melanie) rather than titled (Chapter One: Riding the Double-decker—Andrew; Chapter Two: The Rainbow Cotillion—Melanie). Many readers skip right over chapter titles directly into the chapter text itself. Shocking, I know, but too true.

One **variation** of Alternating POV is Alternating First and Thirds POV, where every other chapter is narrated in First Person by an "I" character (always the same character), and the alternating ones are narrated in Third Person through another character's viewpoint. (Shannon Mayer's intriguing Rylee Adamson paranormal adventure series is a perfect example of Emotional Omniscient Alternating POV using first and third person POVs.)

Alternating POV won't work for every First or Third Person story, but with the right one this format can enhance the story experience for the reader.

# Exercise #6: Emotional Omniscient POV Types—Alternating POVs*

(Purpose of Exercise: To Explore Alternating POVs)

**I'M NOT GOING TO** ask you to produce whole chapters in order to practice this POV type, but I think you can get a feel for how the technique works with this exercise.

Take the scene you have been working with all along. For this exercise I want you to add another character to the two main characters who have been there all the way through. Make this one a bystander, someone who watches what happens between the two main characters. Label the three characters A, B and C in any order you wish. In other words, the protagonist could be character C, the bystander Character A and the antagonist Character B. Or whatever order you choose.

Then rewrite your original scene from Character A's POV, letting the reader see what the character is thinking and feeling. This will be a full Straight Thirds format, with the entire scene from this character's POV. Give yourself **20 MINUTES** to write this full scene.

When you have finished the scene, reset the timer, insert a line break (two blank lines) and continue the scene from Character B's POV. Let this character tell what happens next. Ask yourself: How different is this character from the first? How do the speech patterns vary? How different is the personality, the way of looking at things, the philosophy of life? How does that translate into this character's perception of what happened in the scene, and what happens afterwards? Give yourself **15 MINUTES** for this rewrite.

After you finish Character B's POV of what happened after the first scene ended, insert another line break and switch to Character C. For **15 MINUTES** write the continuation of the story from that person's POV. Ask yourself the same questions as above. Also ask: Does the perspective of this person alter the perception of events a lot or a little? Does this person's POV change the direction of the story? Does it add elements you hadn't consciously thought about before writing?

For an extra challenge, write **the same scene** from the three different points of view: Protagonist, Antagonist and Bystander. Let the scene build to one final conclusion that each character must reach in his/her own way. This technique is fun to use when writing a story about disparate characters who go through the same event (such as a multi-vehicle accident, a fire in a high rise building, etc.) and collide only at the end.

From this exercise, you will come to see how differently each person can interpret the events in which they participate and how easily the main thrust of the events can be twisted out of shape. Misunderstandings and misinformation—and misperceptions—can influence the story's arc. And suspense can be ramped up high when we explore the differing motivations of the main characters and the way those motivations might negatively affect future events. And that tension/suspense is what keeps readers turning pages.

When each chapter is dedicated to a different character who relates his/her own version of the same event, or simply supplies the next portion of the ongoing story, there is ample room for amazing things to happen. With the right story, Alternating POV can be a very effective choice.

# Section 3: Classic Omniscient POV

**CLASSIC OMNISCIENT POV IS** the final type of POV that I uncovered in my search to understand POV. Unlike the Emotional Omniscient POV types, Classic Omniscient does **not** allow the writer to access anyone's thoughts, feelings or emotions.

This poses quite a challenge for a writer. How does one hook readers on characters when they are not privy to their innermost motivations? When all they know is what a camera might see, and a recorder might hear?

Classic Omniscience might not be the right POV Type for most stories, but the challenges inherent in creating a Classic Omniscient story can be definitely worthwhile. Not only because with the right story it makes for compelling reading, but also because not accessing feelings makes the writer pick and choose every word for maximum impact. And that can only make everything a writer writes even better.

# Introduction to Classic Omniscient POV

**THE FINAL TYPE OF** omniscience that writers can use is what I call Classic Omniscience. It is a style of Point of View that has been in use for centuries, and was, indeed, the point of view used in many of the first novels ever written.

Classic Omniscient Point of View is **not an emotional POV**. It uses **no reference to emotions** at all, neither in thought or in accessing the feelings of the characters. It maintains a distance above the action and remains there for the entirety of the story.

Think of a narrator using Classic Omniscient POV as a camera with a voice recorder attached. The narrator reports only what the camera can see and the sounds the recorder can pick up. Nothing more. The narrator **does not access the thoughts or feelings** of any of the characters. No internal thoughts. No memories, unless the character speaks about them aloud. No indication of what is going on inside the character's body other than what can be seen from the outside.

This can at first feel like a very challenging POV in which to write, because we are so used to being able to access our character's thoughts, emotions and inner body reactions to what is happening. We often use those emotions and reactions as a way to hook the reader, to foster sympathy, empathy and curiosity.

The major challenge when you remove the emotion from the POV narrator is building that interest for the reader. We still have to make the characters real and compelling, still have to hook the reader into identifying with at least one character so that they will want to read on and see what happens next. And we have to do it without relying on direct thoughts or on descriptions of what the character is thinking, feeling or remembering.

The secret to a successful story in Classic Omniscient POV is to bring those emotions to the fore **without accessing them directly**. It's a case of, "not what you say, but how you say it." Writers need to choose those details of what can be seen and heard in such a way that it conveys **the impression of emotion**, even though they do not directly access any thoughts, feelings or inner body reactions.

A Classic Omniscient POV story, when well written, can be as effective, moving and compelling as any story written with an Emotional Omniscient POV type. And it's an interesting challenge in choosing exactly the right details, a challenge that, when mastered, helps make all your stories more interesting and appealing to readers everywhere.

# Lesson #7: Classic Omniscient POV

**CLASSIC OMNISCIENCE IS WHAT** I call the final POV type for which the 'experts' cannot agree on a name. In this POV type **the narrator is the source of the Point of View**, not a character in the story. In fact, in Classic Omniscience we never get inside any of the characters' heads at all. We don't know what any of the characters think or feel.

Classic Omniscient Third Person Point of View stands alone, because the Point of View used is not that of a character in the story, but that of a distant, disinterested narrator who hovers above the action and simply describes what is going on. The narrator **does not descend into anyone's head**. Thoughts, feelings and motivations are not part of this type of story, because they are not accessible to the narrator. The narrator is limited to what he can **see and hear only**.

Again, the writer is not the narrator in Classic Omniscience. There is a narrator hovering above the action. The reader hears this narrator's voice, not the voice of a character or of the author. Narrators in this type of story can comment on the action and make guesses and surmises, very much like the Author Intrusion of the past, although they don't usually address the reader directly. But the narrator does not have access to the characters' thoughts, feelings or emotions.

One advantage of Classic Omniscient POV is that the narrator can tell the reader things that the characters can't know or see, or even hear. One example is when the narrator relates something like this:

> Joe and Andrew continued to plan the bank robbery. They didn't know that the police had pulled into the alley and were even now surrounding the building, in which they had planted a listening device.

If this were written in any other POV type, the reader would not know that the police had arrived because the POV character, who would be either Joe or Andrew, could not know it. Nor could they know about the hidden listening device. But a Classic Omniscient narrator, from his position far above the action, has a wider view and can see what is happening outside, around the corner, over the next hill, etc.

Classic Omniscient POV type creates **the most distance** between readers and characters of all the POV types, even more than Second Person POV, because we do not get to know what the characters think and feel about what is happening to them. It takes a lot of skill to create the character/reader bond when emotion is removed from the equation. Like Straight Second Person POV, this type is not often used for novel length works, though in a master's hand it can be quite effective.

Take the example in Lesson #4 (Shifting Thirds). If you remember, this is what it reads like when the writer can dip into the characters' heads.

(Shifting Thirds POV)   Kelly walked into the room on shaky legs, certain that everyone knew what she had done and were hoping to see her stumble and fall. But she had her pride. She'd be damned if she let these old biddies keep her from accepting this award. She lifted her chin and fixed her gaze on the podium as she moved forward.

Janet watched Kelly stalk across the room and felt the breath catch in her throat. She couldn't believe that witch had the nerve to show up. She wanted to intercept her, beat her to a pulp in front of everyone. Janet's hands curled into fists as she fought for control. She looked at Brad, who winked at her, well aware of the emotions roiling inside her. He wondered what she would say if she knew he'd spent last night with Kelly. In her condo. In her bed. He doubted he'd get lucky tonight if Janet found out.

Now let's try it in **Classic Omniscient POV**. Without the emotions, it might read like this:

Kelly walked into the room with her head held high. She did not look at anyone, but kept her gaze on the podium as she walked. People at the tables stopped eating and stared at her. She threaded her way through the tables and approached the steps to the stage, leaving behind her a growing buzz of conversation.

Janet watched Kelly walk across the room. Her brows drew into a frown and her hands curled into fists. She leaned toward Brad, sitting next to her, and spoke while tracking Kelly's progress through the huge, crowded room.

"I can't believe she showed up, after what she did. And I can't believe they're giving her an award. I hope she's booed off the stage."

Brad nodded and gave Janet a wink. But his gaze did not leave the tall, slender figure that approached the steps to the stage.

You can see from this that the emotions and thoughts have been removed. We do not know what the characters are thinking or feeling. The narrator tells us what he sees and lets us hear the spoken dialogue, but does not let us know any of the thoughts, feelings or motivations of any of the characters. All we can do is infer what they might be feeling or thinking from Kelly's body language, the reaction of the crowd, Janet's body language and words and Brad's reaction to Kelly. A skilled writer can infer almost as much emotion in Classic Omniscient POV as in any of the Straight or Emotional Omniscient ones simply though word choice.

But as you read this example of Classic Omnsicient POV, I'm sure you could feel the distance from the characters, more than in any of the other POV types. It often feels as though you are being held at arm's length from the story itself. It is overcoming that distance and hooking the reader that is greatest challenge of this POV Type.

It may not be widely used today, but for some stories, Classic Omniscient POV can be just exactly the right choice.

**READ:** *The Novel Writer's Toolkit* (Mayer, 2003) Page 115, Omniscient Point of View, to Page 117, ending just before Point of View Examples.

# Exercise #7: POV Types— Classic Omniscient POV*

(Purpose of Exercise: To explore Classic Omniscient POV)

**REWRITE YOUR ORIGINAL SCENE** from Lesson #1 using a Classic Omniscient POV; i.e., bouncing around from one character to the other, but never getting into either character's head. Your narration will show **only** the action and what the characters say.

There will be many changes needed to make this POV successful. You will have to pay more attention to details, specific actions, and the words of dialogue, and adjust events where necessary to attain a smooth flow without the emotional aspects of the other Omniscient POV types. And you'll have to be judicious in your word choices in order to imply the emotion that cannot be expressed outright through the characters.

Give yourself **15 MINUTES** to complete this exercise.

# Section 4: Exploring POV

**IT'S ALL WELL AND GOOD KNOWING** the differing types of POV that we can use to tell our tales, but knowing when to use which one is one key to writing stories that readers can't put down. As stated elsewhere, the right POV can lift a good story into a great story.

Experience is the key to truly understanding POV and how to use it to the nth degree. And experience comes from doing what we normally don't do: writing and rewriting the same story in different ways, to see which works best. And then in analyzing the results.

The following exercises are geared to help you do just that: contrast and compare your scenes in differing POV Types, so you begin to gain a visceral feel for the "right" POV. And hopefully these exercises will encourage you to explore a POV change for any story that doesn't quite satisfy you the way it should. There are many reasons stories don't come up to snuff, but POV is usually the last element on a writer's list, if it is even on the list. And yet, sometimes a change of POV—from Straight First Person to Straight Third Person; from Straight Third Person to Third Person Emotional Omniscient; from Straight First Person to a combination of Straight First Person and Third Person, either Straight or Omniscient; etc.—is exactly what the story needs.

The following eight exercises are designed to help you understand the role of POV in your work, and the way POV changes can affect each story. And, hopefully, they will encourage you to move POV a little further up that list of what to check when things aren't going the way they should.

# Lesson #8: Analysis of POV

**WE HAVE NOW EXPLORED** all the different types of POV available to writers today. First, you wrote the same scene in all three of the straight POVs: First, Second and Third. And then you rewrote that scene utilizing the emotional Omniscient POVs: Shifting, Close and Alternating. And lastly, you rewrote the scene one last time in the non-emotional Classic Omniscient POV.

Now that you have had some experience writing these different POVs, it's time to sit down and analyze what you have learned by doing the next seven POV exercises. Only when we fully understand how we, as writers, react to the various POV types, which ones we gravitate to naturally, and which we tend to avoid and why, can we adequately analyze the stories we write to see which POV type will best fit each one.

## Exercise #8: Analyzing the POV Types

(Purpose of Exercise: To analyze our reactions to and understanding of the various POV types we can use for our stories)

**NOW IT'S TIME TO** analyze the seven different POV choices for your original scene. Answer the following questions about your new understanding of POV and the stories you write, or intend to write. **Be sure to tell why** you answer the way you do, because it is in knowing the why of things that we truly learn. Give yourself **30 MINUTES** to write your answers to the following questions.

1. Which POV type was easiest for you to write? Why?
2. Which was hardest for you? Why?
3. Which, if any, did not work for you at all? Why?
4. Which POV allowed you more character development? Why?
5. Which feels richer to you and gives you the most to work with? Why?
6. Which feels most distancing to you, keeps the reader at arm's length from the emotion of the scene? Why?
7. Which POV do you think will pull the reader into the story the most? Why?
8. Which one surprised you the most? Why?
9. Which one stretched you the most, made you think outside the box? Why?
10. If you have already written a few stories, which POV do you currently use the most? Why?
11. If you haven't yet begun to write stories, which do you think you will use the most? Why?

12. Look over any stories you have written or are in the process of writing. Are you satisfied with the POV you chose? Why? Are there any you might change? Why?

13. Think about the stories you are considering writing. Which POV will fit each story? Why? Are there any where you feel you might try more than one to see which will fit best? Why?

14. What do you think are the benefits of experimenting with different POVs when you begin to write a story? Why?

15. Do you think that in the future you will experiment with differing POVs when beginning a story to find the right one? Why or why not?

16. Do you think that in the future you will consider the different types of POV before you begin writing? Why or why not?

17. Will you be willing to rewrite in a different POV if the story isn't working, to see if maybe a POV shift will make it come alive? Why or why not?

18. What kinds of stories do you like to read most? What POV type do the majority of them use?

19. Have ever read a story that didn't work for you? Do you think a POV change would have made it better? Why or why not? If so, which POV do you think would have improved the story? Why?

20. Do you think it would be helpful to write certain scenes from more than one character's POV to see which character is best suited to tell that portion of the story? Why or why not?

21. Now that you understand more about POV and each type's advantages and limitations, do you think you will be more aware of POV problems in the stories and books you read and those you write? Why or why not?

## Future Action:

Spotting POV inconsistencies in the books we read is the first step in spotting inconsistencies of POV in the stories we write. Whenever you find something in a published story that doesn't seem to fit the POV in which it is written, copy it down, noting the POV type in which the story was written. Then analyze what you wrote down to see exactly what the problem is and then figure out how to solve it. By doing this, you will learn to spot inconsistencies in your own work, and will be able to fix them before the story goes into print.

# Lesson #9: It's All In The Attitude

**WHEN WE CREATE CHARACTERS**, we often forget that they are distinctly different from each other. In my first book (still sitting in a drawer—where it belongs) all my characters sounded alike. A reader couldn't have told them apart even by their dialogue. In fact, they all sounded a lot like me!

That is a very common mistake many writers make, especially those beginning to write fiction. They don't realize—or they forget—that characters in fiction are as unique and varied as the people who surround us every day.

One of the problems with writing distinct voices for your characters is that we tend to surround ourselves with people who are like us. They have similar backgrounds, similar education levels, similar hobbies and even jobs. In real life, we tend not to pay much attention to those who are truly different, unless we have no choice. We ignore the way they dress, move, speak, even the way they look at life. And we don't notice the things that are different about our friends and family, because these differences are so familiar to us we no longer see them—

not unless they are glaring dissimilarities that suddenly pop up out of nowhere.

But the characters in our stories are not all the same as us. They are a microcosm of the world in which we live. Each character has his or her own habits, quirks and unique way of viewing the world. Some are pessimists, some optimists. Some believe in God and purpose, some don't. Some are pragmatic, others are dreamers. They all think, act and speak according to their beliefs, their view of the world, the way they were brought up. And each one interprets the events of their lives filtered through the lens of their own life experience.

This is what needs to be translated onto the pages of our stories, the unique perspectives of our point-of-view characters. Without distinctive attitudes, all our characters will sound alike. Readers will not be able to tell them apart. Boredom will set in. The story, no matter how exciting at first, will seem tedious after a while, and they will stop reading. That is something no writer ever wants to happen. Mastering Point of View is one way to guarantee it doesn't.

**READ:** *Write Away* (George, 2004) Chapter 9, Voice: You Gotta Have 'Tude

# Exercise #9: It's All In The Attitude*

(Purpose of Exercise: To find unique, distinctive attitudes and personalities for our POV characters)

**THIS EXERCISE IS DIVIDED** into 4 parts, so it takes longer to complete than the others. All together the 4 parts will take you about an hour or so to finish.

**Part I:** This part of the exercise comes in two steps:

**Step A:** Write a short character analysis of three different characters. You can choose a schoolgirl, a mother, a career woman, a villain, a young man/boy, a father, a famous person, etc. Make them three distinctly different characters from three distinctly different backgrounds. They can know each other, or not, as you choose. (For a real challenge, choose three characters of the same age range with similar backgrounds, or three sisters or brothers or cousins who are close in age.)

In the analysis, concentrate on each character's upbringing, education, prejudices, family history, inclinations and desires, belief systems, career and life goals, etc. You will only have **10 MINUTES per character**, so be sure to concentrate on those attributes that **most** contribute to the character's view of him/herself and the world. Start now.

**Step B:** Now jot down a situation that can be used to create a scene. For example, you could use any of these: a car accident; a purse snatching; a photo shoot; a job interview; a coffee shop where two people bump into each other; a traffic stop by a belligerent cop; etc. All you need here is the situation itself, not the actual scene. Give yourself **1 MINUTE** to note down a situation.

**Part II:** When you finish the character analyses and have your situation, choose one of the characters (Character A) and write a short scene using the situation you chose. Make your scene **mostly narration**, and make sure that the way it is described illustrates the 'voice' of the character. Keep dialogue to a minimum. Start with: *If only she/he had known...* Write for **15 MINUTES**.

**Part III:** Now rewrite the scene with Character B in place of Character A. Concentrate on the second character's 'voice'—his/her biases, way of using language, beliefs that form who that person is. The scene should be exactly the same set up, with the same details, but with Character B in the place of Character A. Only the way events and the setting are described should change. Give yourself **15 MINUTES** for this rewrite, starting now.

**Part IV:** Rewrite the same scene yet again, using Character C's POV and 'voice.' Work to make the language, prejudices, etc, conform to this character's world and self-view. Start now and write for **15 MINUTES**.

When you have finished the three scenes, ask yourself these questions and write down your answers:

Which character's voice did you find it easiest to write? Why?

Which character's voice was hardest to write? Why?

What do you need to know to make that character's voice easier to write?

How much do you think distinct character voices will add to your work if and when you change POVs in a story?

# Lesson #10: Clues to Other Characters' Viewpoints

**IT'S ONE THING TO** talk about Point of View Types and telling a story from one character's perspective. That works well in short stories, mainly because there's not enough time to worry about what's going on in other characters' heads. But in longer pieces like novellas and novels, and even long short stories, readers usually want more than just what one character is thinking and feeling.

Using Close Thirds or Alternating POV helps with that, giving readers large sections or whole chapters of other characters' thoughts and emotions. But often readers want to know what other characters **in the same scene** are thinking and feeling. These clues make readers feel they are there in the midst of the action, watching events unfold. And that keeps them hooked and turning pages.

How can a writer show what's going on in other characters' minds without breaking the rules of POV and slipping into the currently-frowned-upon Shifting Thirds POV? It can be accomplished by using the

POV character's observations and conclusions about what he/she is seeing and experiencing. Sounds simple, but it isn't always.

Consider this excerpt from a story that illustrates either wrong or awkward ways to put in what other characters are thinking and feeling:

> Brad looked up as Joe slid onto the bench on the other side of the table. He frowned. Joe was such a hothead, no sense in that ugly head of his. He remembered the first time something like this had happened, how Joe had lost it, almost landed them in jail. Brad hoped Joe would be able to keep it together this time. He was so scatterbrained, sometimes he gave things away just by the tone of his voice.
>
> "So?" Brad asked.
>
> "It's done." Joe's heart beat a rapid tattoo and his hands shook as excitement surged deep within. "I'm think we got away —"
>
> "Keep your voice down." Brad shook his head. Joe had such a big mouth, he'd spill the beans no matter who was around. "We're not alone in here, you know."
>
> "Who the frig's sober enough to listen?" Joe grinned, then swiveled to leer at the approaching waitress. He was so obviously on edge and high on adrenaline that Brad wanted to hit him.

"Whatcha want?" the waitress said. Her lack of eye contact and the droop of her shoulders gave testimony to how bored she was.

"Beer, baby doll. Draft," Joe said, his eyes skittering over her body as he realized how much he wanted her. Tied to a bed and totally helpless.

He licked his lips and leered more openly. The look reminded Brad of the one Joe had given Shelly that time years ago, and look how that one turned out. Joe on an adrenaline high was a dangerous man, and a careless one. It had taken a lot for Brad to clean up that mess. He hoped he wouldn't have to clean up another of Joe's mistakes. He reached out and squeezed Joe's arm.

This sounds fine, right? Perhaps a bit rough, but you get the idea of what Joe is thinking and feeling from Brad's observations. But there are two mini-flashbacks that aren't necessary and that slow down the action of the scene. And the transitions between the action and the observations feel rather clumsy. Plus there are two POV switches from Brad's POV to Joe's POV. Did you spot them?**

The key to dropping clues is to **keep them subtle** and not let them interfere with the flow of the scene, but rather add to it:

Brad looked up as Joe slid onto the bench on the other side of the table. He frowned when he saw the bright sheen in Joe's beady eyes, felt the manic excitement that rolled off him in waves. This could be trouble, he thought.

"So?" Brad asked, watching Joe's fingers drum a restless tattoo on the tabletop.

"It's done. I'm think we got away—"

"Keep your voice down." Brad shot a look around the dim, smoke-filled room, the sharpness of Joe's voice echoing in his head. "We're not alone in here, you know."

"Who the frig's sober enough to listen?"

The waitress, you a-hole, Brad thought. He shook his head as Joe swiveled to leer at the woman who stopped by their table. The man was obviously riding so high that Brad wanted to haul off and slug him. He never should have brought such a hothead in on this in the first place.

"Whatcha want?" the waitress asked, her tone flat, dead-sounding. Brad could see utter boredom in her lack of eye contact and the droop of her shoulders. He doubted she'd paid attention to what they'd said, not even if they'd shouted in her ear.

"Beer, baby doll. Draft," Joe said in his lazy drawl, the tone Brad knew presaged violence.

He watched Joe's hungry gaze take in the woman's slim body and could picture the dark, sadistic fantasies that rolled through the man's adrenaline-drenched brain. This had all the earmarks of a disaster waiting to happen. He reached out and grabbed Joe's arm, squeezing as hard as he could, enjoying the wince of pain that dampened the dangerous wave Joe was riding.

This version moves along more quickly, with smooth transitions into and out of Brad's observations. Instead of flashbacks that don't add anything other than information that's unnecessary to this scene, we now have hints of Joe's dangerous personality and Brad's uneasiness at having Joe included in whatever the scheme is—hints that compel us to read on to see what will happen. Instead of the graphic thoughts about the waitress from Joe's POV, we have the knowledge that Brad is aware of the darkness in his friend, an awareness that triggers Brad's own darkness to arise. And the entire scene is from Brad's POV, even though we have learned a lot about what Joe might be thinking and feeling.

It takes practice, experience and skill to be able to add clues to other characters' thoughts and feelings without slipping into another character's viewpoint. Most of the time it's easy to figure out how to formulate our sentences so as not to break POV. But sometimes the line gets blurred. The shifts can be very subtle. Even the best writers sometimes break POV without realizing it and it always surprises me when it happens. And it always takes me away from the story for a disconcerting moment or two.

Readers do recognize a POV problem, even a subtle one, though they might not know what to call it. For them, it just feels like something is wrong. Something pulled them out of the story for a beat or two. They might not know what to call it, and they might not understand what POV is, but they do recognize the effect of an unintentional POV switch.

Such switches alert them to the fact that this world, these people and this situation are made up. It's a book they are reading, not a world they have entered to live in for a time. That's not something any writer wants to have happen.

Learning how to give clues to other characters' thoughts and feelings, while remaining in our chosen POV type, is the best way to keep ourselves on track. When we know how to do it right, most of the time we can recognize our slip-ups and fix them ourselves. For those that do elude us, a good critique group can be invaluable for help in locating and eliminating them.

**READ:** *The 38 Most Common Fiction Writing Mistakes* (Bickham, 1992) Chapter 13: Don't Fail To Make The Viewpoint Clear

# Exercise 10: Clues to Other Characters' Viewpoints

(Purpose of Exercise: To find ways to alert readers to other characters' thoughts and emotions without breaking POV)

**PART I.** Write a scene between two people **from one person's point of view**, using the following set-up for your scene. Concentrate on making sure your POV is from **one character only**. Do not put in anything that lets us know directly what the other character is thinking or feeling.

**Scenario:** A man or woman enters an exclusive shoe store looking for very specific shoes for a special occasion. However, his/her feet are unusual in some way: very narrow, extremely wide, very small, very large, etc, and the shoes are outlandish in some way. Write a scene between this person and the shoe salesperson.

Give yourself **20 MINUTES** to write this scene

**PART II.** Now rewrite the scene, adding hints about what the second person in the scene is thinking or feeling, while keeping the scene from the same POV as the first scene. **Do not** slip into the second character's POV. The scene must remain in the first person's POV and only give hints and clues as to what the other person might be thinking and/or feeling.

Give yourself **15 MINUTES** for this rewrite.

\*\*POV switches in the first example above:

1. Joe's heart beat a rapid tattoo and his hands shook as excitement surged deep within. (The scene is from Brad's POV, and he could not know what was going on inside Joe's body.)

2. as he realized how much he wanted her (again, Brad could not know what Joe realized or wanted)

# Lesson #11: First Person or Third Person?

***IT'S A FACT OF*** life—our writing life, that is. We gravitate toward those techniques that we are most familiar with, those that we can write almost with our eyes closed. If most of the books we read and enjoy are written in First Person POV, chances are most of the stories we write will also be in First Person POV. If we most enjoy Third Person POV, we will tend to write our stories from that perspective.

But not all stories can be best told from the POV we instinctively choose first. That choice is most often based not on logical analysis of what is best for the story, but on what we are most familiar with writing. And reading. Sometimes, when a well-written story doesn't quite "sing" off the page the way we hoped it would, the problem is not with the writing, the story line or the plot. Sometimes it is simply rendered in the wrong POV.

Take the beginning of a story I wrote for a contest (didn't win, but that's—as they say—"another story"). I instinctively wrote it in the POV I am most comfortable with, Third Person. Because it is flash fiction short (only 500 words), I stuck with a straight POV. Here is the beginning of the Straight Third Person POV version of the story:

> The milk is all gone. She cannot feed the baby. It will die without food, and she is the source. There must be other options, but from her place chained deep in the dark cave she cannot see any but the one indisputable, immutable fact. The milk is gone.
>
> She holds the frail infant close to her sweating body, fever bright within the deep, moist depths of her being, and she prays to squeeze out one last drop of sustenance for the child. Perhaps osmosis will pass her life into him, though she has only an intuitive grasp of the process. But there is so little life left in her, she has none to spare. Only thoughts remain, an overabundance of words and images crowding her brain: Years of growth and learning; first teeth, first steps, first words of love murmured into another woman's ear. Firsts that now will never be.

I liked this story, but felt that something wasn't quite right. It didn't tug at the heartstrings from the first sentence the way I wanted it to. And it felt a bit manipulative when I read it over.

I sent it to a writing friend, who thought I should try it in First Person POV instead. She thought it would feel more immediate, more desperate, more compelling (Thank you, Sharyl Heber—www.saheber.blogspot.com). That was the first time I had ever thought about rewriting a piece using a different POV. I had always assumed that my first choice was the right one. But I really wanted this story to work, so I did the rewrite (after all, it was only 500 words). Much to my amazement, all it did need was that shift in POV to bring the whole piece to full life. Here is the First Person POV version:

> The milk is all gone. I cannot feed the baby. It will die without food, and I am the source. There must be other options, but from my place chained deep in the dark cave, I cannot see any but the one indisputable, immutable fact. The milk is gone.
>
> I hold the frail infant close to my sweating body, fever bright within the deep, moist depths of my being, and I pray to squeeze out one last drop of sustenance for the child. Perhaps osmosis will pass my life into him, though I have only an intuitive grasp of what that is. But there is so little life left in me, I have none to spare. Only thoughts remain, an overabundance of words and images crowding my brain: Years of growth, of learning; first teeth, first steps, first laugh; the first words of love murmured into a girlfriend's ear. Firsts that now will never be.

As you can see, I didn't need to make many changes other than "she" to "I," especially at the beginning of the story, though as I went further into it there were other alterations that needed to be made because of the POV change. But now the story feels personal. It's immediate. The reader is drawn completely into this woman's world from the very first. There is almost no distance between the character and the reader. That is exactly what this story needed—a change of distance obtained through a change of POV.

It's easy to forget that something as simple as a change in POV from First Person to Third Person, or vice versa, can make all the difference in the impact a piece has on its reading audience. There are so many issues vying for our attention: opening hook, character development, story arc, tension, conflict, dialogue, subplots (if any), climax and resolution, that often POV is overlooked. We reach for the familiar, the comfortable, and leave it at that.

Make sure you consider all the different POV types for each of your stories, and don't make the mistake of assuming your first, instinctive choice is always right. In most instances it will be. But there will be times, like with my story above, when it isn't, when a POV change is exactly what your tale needs to come fully alive.

# Exercise #11: First Person vs Third Person

(Purpose of Exercise: To explore whether a scene is best rendered in First Person or Third Person POV)

***SITUATION: AN ENGAGEMENT PARTY.*** There are three or four major players in this group. You decide who they are and what relationship they have to the engagement. For example, they can be the engaged couple and a former girl/boyfriend, or three bridesmaids, or the parents of the bride and groom, or other friends, relatives, or even the serving staff.

**Part I:** Write about this party, or something that happens during the party, using first person narration from one of the major characters. Make sure to include good tension to keep readers reading on, and stay true to the narrating character's voice. Give yourself **15 MINUTES** to complete this scene.

**Part II:** Rewrite this scene using Third Person POV narration. Use the same character as you did in Part I and have the same things happen, but the narration will now be from third person. This is not just changing all the I's to He or She; the view from the narrator's eyes will change with the change in POV tense. Things may happen in a different way, or be perceived differently, when a narrator enters the picture to tell the story from a character's POV. Different emotions and/or motivations may come to the fore that were not included in the First Person POV version. Take **15 MINUTES** to do this rewrite.

**Part III:** When you finish these two scenes, answer the following questions:
1. Which POV did you find easiest to write? Why?
2. Which POV makes the scene more immediate, more emotion-filled? Why?
3. Which POV do you like the best? Why?
4. If you were writing this story on your own, which POV would you probably have chosen to start out in? Why? Is it different from the one you think is best for this scene?

# Lesson #12: Whose Story Is It, Anyway?

**WHEN WE SIT DOWN** to write, we instinctively choose a character to tell the story, our POV Character. That choice is usually based on what we are comfortable with, and with the way we see the story unfolding in our minds. Even when the idea is still fuzzy around the edges—or even in the center—we feel an affinity with one character above the others. And so we choose that character as the POV character.

But is our instinctive choice always the right one? Consider the Sherlock Holmes stories. Holmes is the main protagonist. It stands to reason that he would be the POV Character of his stories. That would be the logical choice, the one I would have started out with had I written that series. And yet, Conan Doyle chose Holmes' sidekick, Dr. Watson, as the POV narrator of the events that occurred during Holmes' cases.

Why did Conan Doyle do this? For many reasons, the most important of which is the fact that Watson is **the best person to tell what happened.** Holmes was a megalomaniac genius who was addicted to opium. He had a skewed view of who he was, what the world was, and what his place was in it (see: *Unreliable Narrator, Lesson #13*). He suffered from bouts of manic depression and extreme highs. He was not capable of understanding the emotional currents that swirled around his cases, nor was he able to communicate with others on a normal level or to give a rational, coherent depiction of the events that occurred.

Conan Doyle knew that readers would have a tough time connecting with Holmes if they saw him through his own eyes. Given Holmes' shortcomings, had he been the POV Character of each tale, readers would soon have been confused, insulted, and disgusted with the man's arrogance, blindness and intellectual superiority. The only solution was to have Watson, who was in touch with the "real world" and who could humanize Holmes for readers, become the POV Character. He was the best man for the POV Character job.

So what does this tell us? Whether we are writing a Straight POV or an Emotional Omniscient POV story, we need to make sure we are using the correct POV Character to tell the tale. When writing a Straight POV-type story, our first instinct is to have the POV character be the person who the story is about. But, as in the Sherlock Holmes tales, perhaps someone other than our main protagonist may be better able to relate the events that happen. The story could be more interesting from the antagonist's POV. Or more insightful from a friend's or relative's POV. And in an Emotional Omniscient POV-type story, the problem of who should tell which part becomes even more complicated, because we have so many more characters from which to choose.

We need to constantly ask ourselves: **Whose story is this part?** Who can best tell what is happening at this point? Just because the story is about Jenny, who pilfered money from the safe at work so she could buy the registered Persian show cat she'd always fantasized about, doesn't mean she will be the best one to tell the story. Or even the whole story. Maybe her best friend could tell parts that add insights and depth which would lift the story to a new level. Or maybe the police officer who investigates the crime and falls in love with Jenny can add his own unique perspective to certain parts of the story. And taken all together, these differing views will add up to much more than the sum of the parts, and tell a much more engrossing tale than poor Jenny alone could ever do.

Consider one of the scene choices in Exercise #1; for example: the car accident. Your first instinctive choice might be to tell the story from the Point of View of the protagonist, who is driving the car that gets hit. Maybe you once were in an accident, so you can put all the angst and pain and shock into the scene. But maybe the antagonist, behind the wheel in the car that hits the first one, might tell a more interesting side of what happened. Or perhaps a by-stander on the sidewalk, who witnessed the accident, could add a piece of information that is crucial to why the accident happened in the first place, a piece of information that sends the story in a whole other direction.

The point I'm making is two-fold:

1. We don't really know whose POV is the best until we explore what other POV Characters might add to a scene, chapter or story.
2. Exploring other characters' POVs can add depth and interest to a story, and even skew the story in a new, fresher direction than we had first considered.

At every point along the way in our stories, we need to stop and keep asking ourselves: Whose story is it at this point? Who can tell the reader what is really going on in the best, most interesting way? What happy changes might occur if someone else gets to put their two cents' worth into the narrative? Is this really a Straight POV story, or is there room for a more omniscient slant? Or, vice versa, might this omniscient story be better rendered as a Straight POV story?

It is definitely worth taking the time to render a few scenes in different POVs, to make sure that—at that point—you have chosen the very best POV character for that portion of the story.

# *Exercise #12: Whose Story Is It, Anyway?*

(Purpose of Exercise: To learn How to Choose
the Correct POV Character)

**TAKE THE SCENE YOU** worked with for the first 7 Lessons. For this exercise, add another character to the two main characters who have been there all the way through: Character A (protagonist) and Character B (antagonist). Make this one Character C, a bystander, someone who watches what happens between the two main characters. It can be a friend of either Character A or Character B, or a stranger on the street who merely observes what happens. Or someone involved in a way neither Character A nor Character B know about.

Write the scene from Character A's POV, letting the reader see what the character is thinking and feeling. This will be a full Straight First or Third POV format, with the entire scene from this character's POV. Give yourself **20 MINUTES** to write this full scene.

When you have finished the scene, reset the timer and rewrite the scene from Character B's POV. Ask yourself: How different is this character from the first? How do the speech patterns vary? How different is the personality, the way of looking at things, the philosophy of life? How does that translate into this character's perception of what happens in the scene? Give yourself **15 MINUTES** for this rewrite.

After you finish the second character's POV telling of events, switch to Character C, the bystander, and for **15 MINUTES** rewrite the scene from that person's POV. Ask yourself the same questions as above. How does the perspective of someone not involved in the action alter the perception of events? Is the way the scene ends completely different from the way it ends in the first two writings, or is it still the same?

Now read all three versions of this scene and decide who best told the events that occurred. Just whose story was this scene?

# Lesson #13: The Unreliable Narrator

*AN UNRELIABLE NARRATOR CAN* be just what a particular story needs to lift it from the ordinary into the extraordinary.

What is an unreliable narrator? It's a character whose view of the world is so skewed that the reader cannot believe anything he or she says. **Unreliable narrators**—and this is important to remember—**do not know they are lying**. For them, the way they see the world is the absolute truth. Unreliable narrators are supreme egotists, unmitigated pessimists, unparalleled snobs, persons of abject timidity—in other words, confirmed believers in their own twisted version of reality. They interpret events through warped lenses and are convinced that everyone else's view is the distorted one.

Depending on their world view, unreliable narrators might say something like, "Nothing ever goes right for me," just after winning a major prize in a contest, getting married, being promoted to an easier job with a larger salary, being named valedictorian of their class, etc. Or they could color everything with the view, "No one ever does anything right except me," when they are stopped for a traffic violation, called on the carpet for not completing their assignments at work, caught cheating, don't follow directions, etc.

A prime example of an unreliable narrator is the HBO cable TV show, *Dexter*, in which a psychopath who works as a Miami Police forensics expert moonlights as a serial killer of bad people. His world view? These people deserve to be killed because they are murderers themselves who got away with it, so what he does to them is not wrong. He is doing a good deed by committing murder. That he is satisfying his own twisted desire to kill is, for him, beside the point. (The show is based on the Dexter novels written by Jeff Lindsay, the first of which is titled *Darkly Dreaming Dexter*.)

Of course, the reader (or viewer) knows this world view is wrong, and therefore cannot believe anything that Dexter says as he narrates his tales. And therein lies the thrill for the viewer, because some of the things Dexter says really are true. Figuring out which ones becomes addictive.

Most of the suspense in an unreliable narrator story like this comes from trying to figure out what is actually true and what is true only in the narrator's twisted viewpoint. When using an unreliable narrator POV, authors **must be honest** with their readers and **not hold anything back**. The reader needs to know what the POV character knows, just as in any other story. The unreliable stance is not one of trying to deceive the reader, but of **unconscious self-deception** on the part of the POV character.

I once wrote a story about a quilter who made a quilt for her son. No matter what anyone said about the quilt, it didn't matter. To this unreliable narrator, the quilt was a failure because she made one tiny mistake that no one saw unless she pointed it out. The people who exclaimed over its beauty were "blind." The quilt guild members who asked her to teach them her appliqué technique were "deluded." The judges who awarded the quilt a blue ribbon in a county-wide juried show were labeled "incompetent and unprofessional." Her twisted view of the world and her place in it made her unable to see reality as it truly was.

Writing an unreliable narrator story is not easy—one must know the POV character thoroughly and never deviate from the self-deception that is an integral part of the character's makeup—but it can be fun with the right character in the right story.

**READ:** *What If?* (Bernays & Painter, 1990) Page 70, Introduction only

# Exercise #13: The Unreliable Narrator

(Purpose of Exercise: To Write an Unreliable Narrator)

**WRITE A SELF-DECEIVING PORTRAIT** of a character, or narrate a short scene from a self-deceiving character's POV. Remember, these narrators do not see themselves as they really are. They are either more—or less—admirable than the truth of themselves.

Be sure to drop clues to the reader that the narrator is skewing the truth by using subtle signals in language, details, contradictions and biases. The objective is to convince the reader that the narrator's judgment of events and people can't be trusted.

Here is the opening of my story, "Aaron's Quilt," as an example:

Carol hated the quilt; the look of it, the feel of it, the very thought of it. She knew that even if she folded it up and stuck it in a drawer she could never forget it. It would stand as a monument to her stupidity. If so many of her family hadn't known about it, she would have gotten rid of it.

She should have known better than to try to make a quilt. Nothing she did ever turned out quite right. That's all she'd ever wanted, ever since she was a tiny child, to do something, anything, just one thing, exactly right. That's what everyone expected of her, right? And so she listened to both her own inner promptings and her mother—when would she ever grow up?—and embarked on a project that was way beyond her ken. What had she been trying to prove, anyway? Her son was only three, he had no idea what a quilt was. If she just didn't love him so much, if she just didn't want everything to be so special for him, she never would have gotten herself into this fix. But it was done, now, and she would have to live with the consequences.

Her mother first saw the thing when just the top was finished. Carol hadn't had the nerve to try the actual quilting yet.

"Oh, Carol, this is wonderful!" Julia Martin exclaimed.

You can see hints of the unreliable nature of the POV Character, Carol. The exaggeration (a monument to her stupidity), the negativity (nothing ever turned out quite right), the impossibly high expectations (to do just one thing exactly right), the putting blame on other people (if she just didn't love him so much) all point to a skewed view of life and of

Carol's position in it. At first the reader can't be sure Carol is unreliable; she could have made the most awful-looking quilt in fact. But as the reality of the lovely quilt is revealed through the reactions of other people, the reader comes to understand that Carol's view of the world is completely different from what is actually true. She's unreliable.

Now set your timer for **20 MINUTES** and start writing your unreliable narrator scene.

# Lesson #14: Alternating First and Third Person POV

**A FUN VARIATION ON BOTH STRAIGHT** and Omniscient POV can be achieved by mixing both Straight First Person POV with either Straight Third Person POV or Close Thirds Omniscient POV. For those writers, like me, who enjoy writing in both First Person and Third Person POV, this can be especially rewarding, depending on the story.

Of course, you have to be very careful about how you mix these POVs. They have to be specifically structured so that **every POV switch is immediately clear** to your readers. There is great danger in confusing the reader when working this way. And a confused reader will put the book down.

We run an even greater risk of creating this confusion when utilizing Close Thirds Omniscient POV with Straight First Person POV. Close Thirds already consists of line breaks to delineate a change in POV character, shown by the line break. If those breaks are not done with meticulous care, readers can become confused among just the Third Person POV characters' portion of the story.

Then if we add yet another line break to also show a switch into First Person POV, we can totally discombobulate our readers. No matter how skillfully done, a line break switch into First Person POV is usually a startling enough change to cause readers to lose their grasp on just who is telling this portion of the story.

The easiest way to make it fully clear to the reader is to **alternate chapters between First Person POV and Third Person POV** (whether Straight or Omniscient). In other words, Chapter One could be written from the female protagonist's POV in First Person (character A), and Chapter Two from the male protagonist's POV in Third Person (Character B), with a line break toward the end for the POV of the antagonist, also in Third Person (Character C), or even another character (Character D). Then Chapter Three would return to the First Person POV of the female, Chapter Four would relate more of the male protagonist and antagonist's POV from Third Person, and so on.

To put it more clearly:

Chapter 1: First Person, Character A
Chapter 2: Close Thirds, Characters B and C
Chapter 3: First Person, Character A
Chapter 4: Close Thirds, Characters B and D
Chapter 5: First Person, Character A
Chapter 6: Close Thirds, Characters C and D

I am working on a post-apocalyptic, dystopian novel in just such a way. Starting with Chapter One, all uneven numbered chapters (1, 3, 5, etc.) are from Nory's POV in First Person, present tense. All even numbered chapters (2, 4, 6, etc.) are in Third Person Omniscient POV, in past tense, and are shared by three POV characters: Morgan, the weapons maker who saved Nory; Cole, the healer who loves her; and Deerborn, the huntress who fears her. It's a lot of fun switching not only among the characters for their unique POVs, but also alternating between First Person present tense and Close Thirds past tense. And every time readers see sentences like, "I lie here looking across the great chasm of this place where we now live," they know it is Nory. In each Close Thirds section, the sentence immediately after the line break clearly identifies the POV character: "Morgan sat whittling arrows…" "It wasn't the hardest thing Deerborn had done, but it was close," or "Cole checked his supply of elderberry before leaving the compound." By doing this, I can make sure there's no confusion for the reader.

It's extremely imperative, if your alternate chapters are written in Omniscient Close Thirds POV and not in Straight Third Person POV, that you **make sure your POV character is named within the first 2 sentences,** if not the very first. With the switching back and forth between First Person POV and Third Person POV, there is enough going on for your readers. They will thank you (and buy other books you write) for making sure that the text **after every line break** clearly identifies whose POV is now being utilized.

Once readers get the rhythm of the chapters marking not only the POV changes but also the switches from Third to First Person, they will cease to notice them and simply read through the story. If you decide to use Close Thirds POV instead of Straight Third Person in the alternate chapters, those chapters **must use the "rule of three"** for every switch to a new POV:

1) Create a unique, distinct voice for each character;
2) Identify the POV character in the first 2 sentences;
3) Create a line break for each POV switch.

Obviously, not all stories will benefit from this type of Alternating POV. Alternating POV would be hard to work with in a very short story, but novel length ones (though the technique is equally effective for short stories of around 5,000 words or more), can carry an Alternating First Person/Third Person POV with aplomb, as long as the **First Person narrator is the same one** all the way through. Do **not** have multiple First Person POV narrators for the simple reason that it is much harder to identify a First Person narrator by name in the first couple of sentences. People rarely think of themselves by name. Also, try not to have more than 2 or 3 Third Person POV narrating characters who share the alternate chapters, although the same ones do not have to be in all the Third Person chapters. (For a short story, have no more than one Third Person POV character to alternate with the first person narrator.)

# Exercise #14: Alternating First and Third Person POVs

(Purpose of Exercise: To Explore Working with First Person and Third Person POVs in the same story)

**FOR THIS EXERCISE, CREATE** a new scene with two new characters, Character A and Character B. Begin the scene in First Person POV, using Character A as the First Person narrator. Write what happens in the scene in **Character A's voice,** in **First Person** POV narration, until you finish the scene.

Then skip two lines (line break) and continue the story from **Character B's POV**. Only this time you will switch to **Third Person** POV and identify Character B by name within the first two sentences. Continue writing the story until the timer dings.

For example, Character A might be a man who offered a woman he just met a ride home from a club. One thing leads to another and they find themselves out of gas on a deserted road. The first part, written from the man's POV in First Person, and the second part, written from the woman's POV in Third Person, might look like this on either side of the line break:

"Look, lady, I didn't plan this, okay?" I growled at her. "I'm just as unhappy as you about being stranded in the middle of nowhere."

"A likely story." She looked at me as though I were Hannibal Lechter. If looks could kill, I'd be six feet under already. "I know a perv when I see one. And don't think you can keep me here against my will. I have no problem with walking back to town."

I looked at her like I would a cobra getting ready to strike. She'd seemed so stable, so damn nice, back at the club. I could not believe the change in her in the last few minutes. I had no idea where we were, no gas in the tank and no reception on my cell. Just my luck to hook up with a psycho. I should have stayed home and worked on my taxes like I'd wanted to.

"I'm not stopping you," I snarled, not sure who I was angrier with, her or myself. "Go ahead and walk if you think you'll get anywhere."

Gloria slammed the car door behind her just to let him know how pissed she was. The noise bounced around the close-packed trees and made her insides tremble. She couldn't believe she'd let herself fall for his pretty face and sweet manners. She had no business trusting anyone, much less a strange man, not after what had happened years ago at the prom. She took a halting step away from the car. Her knees felt wobbly enough from anger and fright to drop her onto the pavement. She stopped dead.

He put something in my drink! The thought arrowed through her brain and clenched around her heart. She couldn't breathe, couldn't move. It felt like a boulder had risen into her throat. Her stomach heaved and she feared she would vomit. No wonder she felt so shaky. Good thing she hadn't finished the one drink he'd bought her. That was probably why she was still conscious and on her feet, shaky though she felt.

She turned to look back at him just as he clicked on the penlight that dangled from his car keys. She could see his face clear as day, see the calculation that flooded his eyes, the evil that rolled off him like a dark cloud. Her worst nightmare was about to come true. It was the prom all over again. Then he moved, reached for his door handle. She turned and ran back the way they'd come as fast as she could in her stupid stiletto heels.

Set your timer for **30 MINUTES** and begin writing. Remember to leave 2 blank lines between the two POVs.

# Lesson #15: Spotting and Correcting POV Inconsistencies

**LEARNING TO SPOT POV** inconsistencies, not only as we write but also as we read, is an invaluable skill writers need to cultivate. Keep a notebook beside you as you read and note down any POV problems you find. Copy out the text where the problem is embedded so you can refer to it later, and note also the POV type the author used in writing the piece. Then, when you're back at your computer, you can take the excerpt and analyze it to find where it went wrong. And you can rewrite the problem area for yourself, to see how it could be corrected.

Once we, as readers, are aware of POV inconsistencies, we can usually spot them fairly quickly, even the subtle ones. We may need to think about those—what caused them, why they pulled us from the story—but with practice we can become adept at spotting the areas that don't quite work.

Why is this important? Because the more easily we can spot (and correct) POV inconsistencies when we read, the more easily we can spot them when we inadvertently write them into our own work. And trust me, we will. Quite often a first draft will be riddled with all sorts of problems, POV switches among them. That's why we rewrite and rewrite, again and again. However, the more familiar we become with the many ways those inconsistencies creep into our writing, the faster we can spot and correct them—often while we are still writing that first draft. And that means we can concentrate more fully on character development, story arc and plot in future drafts, and less on the mechanics of the writing. And that makes for a stronger story that readers are sure to enjoy.

## Exercise #15: Spotting and Correcting POV Inconsistencies

(Purpose of Exercise: To Learn to Spot and Correct POV Inconsistencies)

**THE FOLLOWING EXAMPLES OF POV** inconsistencies were written especially for this book, by some very fine writers with whom I work. Each author **deliberately** added a POV error or two to the selection. Read each one, note the type of POV used and try to spot the flaw(s) in the POV. Then rewrite the short piece so that the flaw is corrected.

Do the same with every unfounded POV switch you encounter in the books you read. You might even find yourself eventually able to spot the flaw and correct it in your head without putting the book down.

If you do this every time you read, you will develop the ability to spot even the smallest, most subtle of inconsistencies in your own writing. You'll also be able to more easily spot them in the work of fellow writers in your critique groups. And you'll find your writing becoming all the stronger for that knowledge.

And keep in mind that each of these examples were written to specifically have a POV inconsistency in them, expressly for this exercise.

**Example #1:** From author Laurie Woodward: www.artania.com

I walked in the shadow of the neon forest for hours, eyes blinking in bewilderment. Recognizing nothing. Not a single street or building was familiar. How long had I been watching the trash shuffle beneath my feet? Where had this journey begun? Did it even have a beginning?

Off in the distance I heard someone humming and surprised myself by joining in. I was somehow drawn to the ephemeral music. My shadow bounced ahead of me as I moved toward the sound. Beneath the yellow spotlight of a used car lot a second shadow joined my own.

I drew closer to the figure and slowed. Wire-rimmed spectacles reflected a fugue of light that momentarily blinded me. I faltered and would have fallen had it not been for the outstretched arms of my spot-lit partner.

"Aye, bloke. Stumbling again, are we?" asked the Stranger. He had waited long for the Lost One's return and felt neon bubbles coursing through each vein at his touch.

"I couldn't see." I replied. "Your glasses. They were so bright. A kaleidoscope of color."

**Example #2:** From Sue McGinty's new Bella Kowalski mystery, "Murder in Mariposa Bay." www.suemcginty.com

Pisniak tears the application for campground handyman in two, deposits it in the recycle bin and grinds his cigarette into the dirt with the toe of his boot. He lowers the cap over his eyes, then thinks better of it and hides it in the trash beneath a paper bag. Goodbye, old friend. Head down, eyes averted, he hurries to his pickup.

Because his eyes are focused elsewhere, the man once known as Steve Pisniak doesn't see his former friend peer over the top of his newspaper, doesn't notice the Escalade parked near the restroom, doesn't observe the old geezer behind the wheel put a cell phone to his ear, doesn't hear the call that will end his life.

**Example #3:** From author Mark Arnold (markarnoldphd@gmail.com)

"Please Kyle!" *I have to hear it*, she thought, fighting to catch her breath. "Please!"

Kyle drew back. "What?"

"I have to know. Do you love me?" She sounded like a hungry kitten.

Every time in every relationship there is that moment, the one when they wanted more than a gesture, more than dedication, more than commitment. There was the moment you had to say, The Word.

"You know I do." More kisses, and more, and . . .

"Please Kyle!" Again, I voiced the breathless request as old as time. "Say it!"

Kyle tried to focus inside the faintly musty scent of back-seat fabric, the pounding rain on the roof of the car, the slickness of the steamy windows where bare hands and feet fighting for purchase slid and squeaked.

"Oh, baby, listen with your heart." *Sincerity. Yeah that's it.*

**Example #4:** From Tony Piazza (www.authortonypiazza.com)

Paris is the city of romance, or so they say. Not for this journalist. On this occasion I was sitting at a sidewalk café watching a couple across the aisle whispering sweet endearments to each other. Depressed, I sipped on my espresso, gazing sullenly up at the gray sky and then down towards the featureless crowds that passed before me. Loneliness had now reached my soul, an emptiness as barren as the trees which lined the boulevard along the Seine, and as hollow as the taps of gentle rain hitting the awning above me.

"Is this seat taken?" A woman suddenly asked, her request taking me by surprise.

"Please," I offered. My first glance saw that she was charming, and she likewise studied my face and thought that she had finally found the kind of man she'd been searching for.

**Example #5:** From Tony Piazza (www.authortonypiazza.com)

The old man slipped off the burro and wandered aimlessly towards the mounds of sand that filled his horizon. He stumbled a few times on his way, but always seemed to pick himself up—an outward sign of his firm determination. I may have been delirious from the heat, or just driven mad by my lust for the gold, but for whatever reason I just kept moving ahead even if I hadn't any real destination in mind.

**Example #6:** From Susan Tuttle's soon-to-be-released mystery, "Piece By Piece," (www.SusanTuttleWrites.com)

The phone rang, shattering the early morning silence. Ogden Wilkes glanced at the clock as he snatched up the receiver. 4:10 am. He knew it had to be more than important. Only the wounding of one of his men was serious enough to drag the precinct captain out of his comfortable bed.

He held the phone to his chest a moment, waiting until his heart slowed and his mind began working again. The events of the last thirty-six hours filtered through his consciousness and he was amazed that he'd actually fallen asleep. His wife, Judy, awakened by the ring, muttered an incoherent sound and turned over, put her back to him. Wilkes inched his way to the padded headboard and brought the receiver to his ear.

"Yes, what is it?" His quiet voice seemed to echo in the still room.

His dog, Musuko, asleep on the floor under the partially open window, sat up, ears alert, paws restless on the carpet, eager to share in the nighttime excitement.

"Traynor here, Captain. I'm with Selling, in an alley down by the river, between Fourth and Lexington. I think you'd better get down here."

"Who is it?" Wilkes threw back the covers and swung his feet to the floor.

"Cliff Davisson."

(The POV inconsistencies and ways to fix them are detailed at the end of the following section, so you can check your work against the answer key.)

# Examples From My Class Writing

When I teach my "What if" Writing Group classes, I don't just stand at the front of the room and instruct. I also participate, doing each of the exercises with my students. I do this for a number of reasons, not the least of which is that I, too, still have much to learn about writing. But I also do it to help my students understand and analyze their own work by giving them something written by a published author/professional editor against which to compare it.

This is not to say that what I write is always perfect; there are times when it falls short of the mark, when I could have done much better. Still, I thought that some of you might want a little of what I produce in the classes as clarifying examples in case of confusion, or to use as a yardstick against which to measure your understanding of the lessons, since we're not able to share face-to-face. Just be aware that of what follows, nothing is edited, tweaked or polished. Everything is a product of timed writing sessions done during my actual classes.

# Lesson #1: Straight First Person POV

I walk into the room with my head held high. I'm wearing the red dress, the one that cost almost a month's salary. It contrasts nicely with my dark hair, and shows off what the papers have called my "luscious curves" the way everyone has come to expect they will be shown. Image is important. And tonight, it's everything.

I came late on purpose. There's no sense making an entrance unless all eyes can fasten on you. And this is an entrance par excellence, a nose-thumbing, in-your-face, up-yours entrance if there ever was one. I pause just inside the door, barely over the sill, balancing on my stilettos like a cat on a high wire, and let them all have a good long look.

I know what they are thinking, especially Margot. What the hell am I doing here? How could I have the nerve to show up after what I did? Only thing is, I didn't do anything. Not that any of them would believe that. Tried and convicted by public opinion is steel set in cement. Nothing short of an atomic blast can remove it from their minds.

I give my hips a little room to sway as I stalk across the room toward the stage. Silence ripples before me, and murmurs close in behind. I think of what fun it would be to stare them all down, self-righteous prigs that they are, but I spot Margot sitting like a queen at the station's table and I know the night just got harder to live through.

Maybe I shouldn't have come, I think. A droplet of fear arrows through me as I wonder what she will do. She's a hothead, unpredictable, and the one who spread the rumors about what happened. Of course, she was out of town at the time so she has no direct knowledge, but that didn't stop her tongue. It started wagging the moment she learned about what happened to Caden, and hasn't stopped yet. I don't think I've ever hated anyone as much as I hate her, not even Caden himself.

I let my lips drift up into a smirk and give her my disdainful sideways glance, the one I've perfected over the last few weeks to deal with intrusive media underlings. I know that will only rile her, as does my presence here, but I don't care. We've been angling toward blows for three weeks now. What better place to allow it to come to fruition than a room full of media executives? My picture's already graced the papers more than I like. What's one more inconvenient photo on page one?

Margot's face changes. Her supercilious smile hardens into a sneer and her eyes spit fire. She leans over to Craig and says something, her gesture one of dismissal. He looks over his shoulder at me and his eyes widen. Do I see a flash of approval in them? is he actually happy I came to receive the award in person?

Then Margot starts to rise and Craig grasps her arm. She shrugs him off and gains her feet. Before he can reach out again to stop her, she's halfway to me. Deep silence falls as she stops in front of me. We stand in an oasis, a vacuum, eye to eye.

## Lesson #2: Straight Second Person POV

You walk into the room with your head held high. You have the red dress on, the one that cost more than you could afford. But you know what it does for you, for your body. It's a statement you want to make, this night of all nights.

You pause just inside the doorway, for maximum effect. You're late, because why make an entrance if it's not a show stopping one? And you need an entrance tonight, just like you need this just-barely-a-slut dress.

It's a symbolic thumb-your-nose gesture, and though you're quivering inside, wondering what will happen, your heart thrills to the danger and uncertainty.

You know what's going through their minds as they look you over; what they think of you, what they think you've done. Especially Margot. The funny thing is you've done nothing, at least not what they believe you capable of. It's that more than anything that hurts, that they believe you capable of such duplicity. Well, let them look, you think, letting a smirk lift your lips. Let them believe what they want. You don't care. Not tonight. This is your night and no one can take that from you.

You step forward on your fuck-me stilettos, well aware of how your hips sway and entice as you walk into the room. Silence falls as you approach and you wonder if anyone will accost you, throw their thoughts in your face. But no one even looks directly at you. They glance from the corners of their eyes and turn their heads, and your heart stutters. Do not stop, you tell yourself as your pace slows. They are not worth the price of the paper they're printed on.

But you know that isn't true. These people were your friends, or so you thought. They all voted for you, voted to award this honor on you. Of course, that was before Margot's slimy little rumor made the rounds and they all turned against you. Now they are wondering why you are here, how you have the nerve to show your face. After what happened to Caden they all turned their backs. Not one of them so much as asked you what happened, if it was true, much less stood up for you, refused to believe you capable of such treachery.

Well, you tell yourself as murmurs close in behind you, who needs friends? They are talking about you and you want to turn and scream at them. But then you see Margot, sitting at the head table like a queen lording it over her subjects, and your spine stiffens. The disdain in her eyes shudders into you and you wonder if you can pull this off even as your feet change direction, veer toward the steps up to the stage.

You give her your sideways glance, the one you perfected in the mirror, the one that says "you're of no account." And you can't help but smile as her expression freezes, then sifts into glittering anger. She starts to rise but Craig, sitting next to her, grabs her arm and holds her in place. She turns to him, and you watch her gesture to him, the meaning clear: She wants you gone.

## Lesson #3: Straight Third Person POV

Jayelle stopped in the door to the banquet room and struck the pose she'd practiced all week: A disdainful siren come to accept the accolades of her inferiors. The momentary pause gave her time to gather her courage for the ordeal ahead. And it allowed the occupants of the room—her so-called colleagues—time to absorb her presence, to realize that, no matter what they thought of her, they couldn't run her out of town.

She let a smirk play on her lips, capping off her statement of disdain and haughteur. She'd dressed carefully for the occasion, for maximum effect. Her violently red dress fitted her lanky curves like a glove and left nothing to the imagination. Not even the price tag, which was good since it cost more than two weeks' salary. jayelle knew the contrast of the vibrant color with her dark hair and eyes only enhanced the image she wanted to portray: a victor in seductress clothing. After all, in her world image was everything. Especially tonight of all nights.

After a long moment she took a deep breath and sashayed into the room. She could feel her hips sway as she stepped out on her glittering stiletto heels and wondered how much of the silence that greeted her was caused by the image, and how much by what they were thinking. *Don't kid yourself*, she thought. *The image might have shocked them, but it's your presence that has struck them dumb.*

She glanced at the tables as she passed each one on her journey to the stage, but no one would look at her. not directly, anyway. She was well aware of the sideways glances her progress evoked. And the way a low murmur grew as she left each table in her wake. *Cowards,* she thought, refusing to give in to the pain searing her heart. Not one of them had stood up for her, not one of them had questioned or challenged Margot's rumors about what she'd done to Caden. They simply accepted the bitch's vitriol as gospel truth and turned their backs as one. All her friends.

*Who needs friends?* she thought now, tilting her head to send an ironic smile toward Kristianne, once her bosom confidante. Kristianne's face reddened and she turned her head away. *Friends are just an opportunity to garner pain.*

Jayelle continued on toward the stage, though what she really wanted to do was turn and scream at all of them. Take them down off their self-righteous pegs, grind them into the floor with shame and misery. But she knew it would do no good. Their minds were made up, She'd been tried and convicted in the court of popular opinion. The verdict, regardless of the truth, was set in steel-reinforced concrete that only an atomic blast could eradicate.

She glanced up and spotted Margot at the head table, sitting like a queen lording it over her subjects. Margot of the evil tongue. Jayelle shuddered and almost stopped. But Margot looked up and saw her. Jayelle watched disbelief flood her face, followed by ice-cold anger that glittered from Margot's green eyes and rolled off her in waves of antagonism. She started to rise and Jayelle wondered if she would rush down the steps and attack her in front of everyone. She'd been threatening to do so if Jayelle had the nerve to show up at the awards ceremony. That challenge was the one that had brought her here tonight.

She smirked at Margot as her feet veered her toward the steps. Craig, sitting beside her, reached for her arm and held her down. Jayelle watched as she turned to Craig, her hands gesturing. The meaning was clear to Jayelle, and probably everyone else watching the show: Margot wanted her gone.

# Lesson #4: Emotional Omniscient POV - Shifting

Meleia looked at Menja Solon as he stood blocking the cell door. He stood with legs spread, arms folded, like a stone statue, she thought, or an immovable block of wood. An intimidating pose, she knew, and though her heart quivered and her body trembled, she lifted her head, refusing to let him know just how frightened she was.

Solon smiled to himself. This little chit of a girl was so transparent, he could almost see through her skin and muscle to her clenched stomach and fluttering heart. Though she hid it well, he'd give her that. He let his gaze caress her lifted chin and wished she were older. Despite his unearned reputation, little girls didn't interest him. But this one...

"What do you want with me?"

Melia's voice rang clear in the dank air of the cell. Solon smiled in appreciation of her courage, foolish though it was. Meleia lifted her gaze to his, determined to foil whatever plans he had.

"Just you, my dear," he said, his voice a deceptive purr. "Just you."

Melia clenched her hands as she looked into her captor's icy, speculative eyes. She'd thought his pursuit and her capture just another ploy in averting her destiny, a destiny she didn't even want. But it seemed now that there were more destinies from which to choose, and this wasn't one she'd accept on any terms. If Menja Solon thought to force her, he'd find his task an impossible one. She braced herself to fight off an adversary larger and stronger than she was, knowing she had a weapon of which he had no knowledge.

Solon's eyes widened as he read Meleia's thoughts, so clear in her eyes. What was she hiding? She didn't show enough fear, not by half. By now she should be groveling at his feet, pleading for mercy. instead she stood tall and determined, and sure of her success should they tangle. Perhaps she truly was The One they awaited. Perhaps the old sorceress hadn't steered him wrong. He dropped his gaze down the length of her body and Meleia almost smiled, knowing she'd shaken him to his core.

## Lesson #5: Emotional Omniscient - Close Thirds

Meleia looked at Menja Solon as he stood blocking the cell door. Her captor. He stood with legs spread, arms folded, like a stone statue, she thought, or an immovable block of wood. An intimidating pose, she knew, and though her heart quivered and her body trembled, she lifted her head, refusing to let him know just how frightened she was.

Solon smiled at her and once again her heart stuttered. She didn't like the speculative look in his eyes, the way his gaze seemed to penetrate deep within her. She tightened her lips and dared him to come closer. Just one step, that's all she wanted. Then she could beat him into the ground.

"What do you want with me?"

Melia's voice rang clear in the dank air of the cell. She watched a slow smile lift his lips and she wondered if her defiance amused him. *Don't get too cocky, you creep*, she thought, tilting her head. His jaw worked and she was sure he could read her thoughts. His smile widened.

"Just you, my dear," he said, his voice a deceptive purr. "Just you."

Melia clenched her hands as she looked into her captor's icy, speculative eyes. She'd thought his pursuit and her capture just another ploy in averting her destiny, a destiny she didn't even want. But it seemed now that there were more destinies from which to choose, and this wasn't one she'd accept on any terms. If Menja Solon thought to force her, he'd find his task an impossible one. She braced herself to fight off an adversary larger and stronger than she was, knowing she had a weapon of which he had no knowledge.

Solon's eyes widened and he seemed to hold his breath. Meleia could see thoughts race behind his eyes, though she had no idea what they were. His stance shifted, an almost imperceptible change she wouldn't have caught if she hadn't been watching him so closely. Did he now understand who she was, what she was here for? Did he at last understand what she was capable of? He dropped his gaze down the length of her body and Meleia almost smiled, knowing she'd shaken him to his core.

***

Menja Solon stared at the young girl who stood so defiantly in the dank, dim cell. His eyes widened as he read her thoughts, so clear in her lovely violet eyes. She was hiding something, he knew. What? She didn't show enough fear, not by half. He'd given her enough signs for her to assume he wanted her body beneath him; he'd carefully cultivated that erroneous image to strike fear into most women's souls, though little girls really didn't interest him. The fear, and what it brought him, that was what he was after.

By now she should be groveling at his feet, pleading for mercy. instead she stood tall and determined, and sure of her success should they tangle. Perhaps she truly was The One they awaited. Perhaps the old sorcerthess hadn't steered him wrong.

Could it be? He again dropped his gaze down the length of her body and felt his center shift, his priorities rearrange. If this was The One, he needed to bind her to him, make her dependent on him. What he needed was to become her protector, her adviser, her mentor. A father figure, one she would trust above all others. Then he could twist her, use her for his own ends.

*You're a fool*, he thought. He'd killed her companions, captured her, hit her and bound her, then brought her here to his dungeon where he'd all but promised to take her against her will. And now he had to make her trust him?

He almost gave up, almost turned away. If he kept her locked away, let her rot in here, then destiny would be foiled. Life would't change. He might not get what he wanted, what he knew he was due, but then neither would anyone else. No one would know The One sat in his dungeon, below his very feet. Destiny would be his to rule, not hers.

He grinned and took a step forward. Meleia raised her hands. And the cell exploded around him.

## Lesson #6: Emotional Omniscient POV - Alternating

The first part of this exercise is the end of a chapter; the second part is the beginning of the next chapter. I chose to render the last scene of the first chapter once again in the following chapter from a different character's point of view, because both Meleia's and Solon's views are important here.

**End of First Chapter:**

Meleia sat atop Creven, using her hands and legs to control the restless stallion as she stared across the valley. Somehow, they had to cross that vast open plain and still evade the army Narwah had sent after them. And she still didn't trust Menja Solon, who rode beside her through this land. Though he'd seemed to understand who she was, what her mission was, he was still too caught up in his own agenda for her to give him complete control of her safety. And that left only Emril, the chandler.

*Great choices*, she thought. *Why isn't anything ever easy?*

She turned away and rode back into the camp. Emril stood over the fire, stirring something in the cauldron. Solon sat studying the map the old Sorcerer had given them the night before. Solon appeared to have complete confidence in the oily little man, but Meleia had been betrayed too often, and by people who seemed at first to want to help. No way was she trusting someone who would send them across an expanse of flat land with nowhere to hide. And nowhere to shelter at night.

"We're not going this way," she said. Menja Solon looked up at her as she dismounted.

"This is the way Gaffan said we had to go."

He looked at her with hooded amber eyes, those disconcerting eyes she couldn't read. Except when he wanted her to. She saw Emril stop stirring. He stood stone still, not looking at them, but not looking away, either.

"It's too open." Meleia hobbled Creven and left him nibbling the sweet grass that covered the trail that led out of the forest, then walked toward Solon. "Not safe enough."

"There's no other way." Solon stood, map in hand. "Gaffan wouldn't steer us wrong."

"Everyone and his mother would steer us wrong if it got them on the good side of Narwah. I don't trust him enough to cross that plain at night, much less in the daytime."

Solon crossed his arms and glared at her. She wondered if he really would try to tie her up and drag her unwilling carcass with him over that open meadow, the way he'd threatened to last night. Emril dropped the ladle in the cauldron and took a step toward them.

"Solon," he said, his low voice filled with menace.

"Lord Solon to you, boy," Solon growled. He tilted his chin but did not take his unnerving eyes off Meleia. Her heart began to thud.

From the corner of her eye she saw Emril stiffen. His hand dropped to where the knife sat sheathed at his waist. He took another step forward.

Then Drinn appeared from the dense forest and stalked into the center of the trio. Dried leaves clung to his silky coat. Cobwebs united his whiskers. He wound around Emril's feet, then undulated over to sit beside Meleia. His back stretched, his limbs elongated. Wings sprouted from his spotted back. His purr turned to a growl and he stared back into the woods from where he'd come.

'They're here,' Meleia heard in her head, her heart. 'Run.'

## Start of Second Chapter

Menja Solon sat studying the map old Gaffan had conjured the night before. He'd trust that Sorcerer with his life, but he wasn't sure he'd trust him with Meleia's. She was so much more important than he'd first thought. In his arrogance he had thought he could use her for his own ends. He still mourned his grand plans. It wasn't easy living in an end time, even if what was coming would be beyond anything he could imagine.

He traced the route Gaffan had indicated, his nail leaving a faint glow behind, a thin line of luminescence that seemed somehow a benediction. He could feel it begin, the inner stirrings of his soul that presaged a premonition. He closed his eyes, attempting to bring the vision into clarity.

"We're not going this way."

Meleia's voice sliced through his concentration. He hadn't been aware she had returned, hadn't even heard Creven's heavy clops on the hard ground. Frell, he had to get himself in hand.

"It's the way Gaffan said to go."

He looked up at her. His heart jerked at the way her face glowed in the morning light. She stooped to hobble Creven then walked over to stare him down, her expression stubborn and sullen. Again Solon's heart jerked.

"It's too open. Not safe enough," she said as though she had control of where they went. But she didn't. This was his land, his home. He was lord here, not this chit of a girl, no matter who she said she was. Solon's hackles began to rise.

"There's no other way. Gaffan wouldn't steer us wrong," he said, keeping his voice deceptively soft. He didn't even believe what he was saying, he just knew he had to gain control over this situation, fast. There was too much at stake to let Meleia think she could escape Narwah's army on her own wits.

"Everyone and his mother would steer us wrong if it got them on Narwah's good side," she said and took a step toward him, her hands fisted. He longed to grab her and shake some sense into her. What did she think prophesy was? Fodder for novels and stories to scare little children with?

"I don't trust Gaffan enough to follow his supposedly sage advice at night much less in the daytime."

Solon watched Meleia lift her chin and dig in her heels. He'd probably have to tie her up and sling her across his saddle to get her going where they needed to go. His hands began to itch.

"Solon."

Frell! It was her puny sidekick. He'd forgotten about Emril, the servant turned bodyguard. As if the idiot could wield a sword well enough to to cut his own head off. The one-time chandler took a step toward Solon, his hand hovering just over the knife sheathed at his waist. Gods, would he have to fight that moron, too?

Motion at the corner of his eye caught his attention. Drinn stalked out of the forest. Dried leaves stuck to its slinky body and cobwebs draped from its whiskers. Solon hated the gargoyle, even in its cat form. It was all he could do not to move his feet as the fey feline strutted past him to Emril. It wound around Emril's legs, then sauntered over to settle beside Meleia. As Solon watched it began to morph. Its back elongated, its limbs stretched out. Scales began to replace its silky black fur. Wings sprouted from its shoulder blades. Solon's hand tightened on his sword hilt. How he'd love to run that thing through!

Then Meleia's eyes widened and Solon realized the thing growing at her side had spoken to her. And that, he knew, meant trouble headed their way.

## Lesson #7: Classic Omniscient POV

As you read this piece, look for places where I used visual and auditory clues to the emotions and thoughts of the characters.

J.C walked into the room and looked around. Little was visible in the dimness. Only one candle burned in a far corner. Cobwebs draped in the corners and depended from the iron candelabra that hung from the center beam, its sockets empty. The front and side walls were rough-hewn boards, but stone gleamed along the expanse of the back wall. Wax coated the floor beneath the empty fixture. J.C.'s foot slipped as he stepped across it. He windmilled his arms and lurched to the side, but kept his feet beneath him.

"Do you think this is where he held her?" Andrew stood in the doorway, squinting.

"Could be," J.C. answered. He approached a small side table that stood against the left wall. "We'll know only if we find some evidence." He turned and looked at Andrew, his head cocked, one brow lifted. "Care to join in the fun, partner?"

Andrew grunted and moved toward the right side of the room. An iron rack stood in the shadows, barely discernible. Oddly shaped items hung from chains attached to the top cross bar. Andrew reached up and touched them, one by one, his movement slowing as he moved from right to left. He reached the final object, one ring of a handcuff set, and snatched back his hand. He looked at his fingers. His lip lifted. His eyes scrinched almost closed. his gasp echoed loud in the empty room.

"What is is?" J.C. asked.

"There's something here. I don't think you're gonna like it."

J.C. strode over to Andrew and looked at his hand.

"Looks like blood to me," he said, turning to look at the soiled handcuff.

"Yeah, it does."

"We need a flashlight. Damn! If the car hadn't gone in the river... Well, we'll do the best we can until the C.I. Unit gets here."

J.C. pulled a pair of latex gloves from his pocket and put them on. Then he examined each of the items hanging from the top bar, squinting in the dim light. Two three-foot lengths of chain ended in sharp, barbed hooks, both of them stained dark. Three wires dangled a foot off the floor. J.C. knelt and slid his hand low along the wall. A battery pack was attached to a board tucked into the far back corner. toggles stuck up from the board. J.C.s eyes narrowed as he stood and dusted off the knees of his pants.

"It'll be her blood, I'll bet a year's salary. This is where the bastard kept her." He pointed as he spoke. "He cuffed her to the rack, tortured her with the hooks, shocked her with the wires." His jaw worked and his body tensed, muscle and sinew bulging as he waved down the length of the iron contraption. "I don't even want to think about what he did with those other things."

Andrew shuddered and closed his eyes. J.C. paced across the room, head bent and turning from side to side. Andrew backed away from the torture rack, quick breaths lifting his chest. Then he turned and watched J.C. for a moment.

"Anything?" he asked.

"Can't tell," J.c. said, walking parallel to the left wall, heading toward the back of the room, in the direction of the burning candle, "not without more light. But given what w've found so far, I'd say there's probably a lot to find here."

"Where do you think he's taken her? If she's still alive..."

J.C. didn't answer. He stood staring at the back wall a moment, then lifted his fist and smashed it into the cold stone. He growled and cradled his hand on his left arm.

"Oh, smart, partner, real smart," Andrew said.

J.C, turned, his face red, and opened his mouth. He froze. In the distance, sirens wailed, drew closer. Both men looked at each other, then moved toward the door.

## Lesson #9: It's All In The Attitude

Can you figure out who these characters are just from the scenes? (Answers at the end of the three scenes.)

**Situation:** On a game show, competing for a cash prize of $10K.

### Scene with Character #1:

If only Joelle had known the outcome of the day, she never would have agreed to be on the show.

"we'll start the final round in just a few minutes," the emcee, Jack Haney, said. "Is everyone clear on the process?"

They all nodded, even Joelle, although she wasn't really sure about what would happen. She knew it meant matching things, names with titles of books, and she would be good at that. Her mother taught her all sorts of stuff she'd never need on the farm, but Mamma wanted her well rounded, whatever that meant. All that knowledge hadn't helped her when she did go to school, the kids seemed to resent her for it. But the teachers thought it was wonderful and that made Joelle happy.

"Five!" the director called out. "Four..." then he counted down on his fingers, three, two, one and pointed to Jack, who went into his spiel. Suddenly, before Joelle realized, it was time o spin the wheel. The other two contestants had already spun it and achieved numbers of 7 and 4 respectively. Joelle felt pleased for the mother of three who had gotten the 7. That meant she'd go first, and maybe win a lot of money. She could use it with three kids at home, and a husband in the marines.

"Joelle, it's your turn to spin," Haney said.

Joelle leaned down and grabbed the wheel, gave it a shove. It spun while Joelle watched and thought about Marylou winning money for her children. The wheel stopped on 9. Joelle had won the first turn. She blinked, both disappointed and pleased. Disappointed that Marylou had lost het first-turn advantage, and pleased that she had won it.

Life is just such a kick, she thought as the blank board at the back of the stage revealed her question. The title of a book stood at the top: ***As Beauty Does***. Below it were four names, out of which she had to pick the author: Grace Meridian; Joseph Kellerman; Sharyl Heber; and Ronald Rosin.

Joelle hadn't read this book. It must have come out after her mother died, after she'd stopped reading for pleasure and had to read to please teachers in the public school. *This will make winning even more exciting, if I do win*, she thought. it wouldn't be quite the feat it should be if she knew the answer ahead of time. She grinned at the studio audience, her heart thudding in anticipation. *Think it out*, she thought. *If you win you can always share it with Marylou and her kids.*

It wouldn't be a man who wrote it, not with a title like that. So she had a 50/50 chance. When she thought about it, someone named Grace would have to be very arrogant to use the word 'beauty' in her title.

"Ten seconds, Joelle. Who's the author?" Haney asked.

Joelle crossed her fingers and made her guess.

"Sharyl Heber."

Confetti rained down from above. The audience cheered and applauded. Jack Haney pumped her hand, his words lost in the din. He handed her a huge check, made out with her name in the amount of $10,000.00. Tears flooded her eyes. She turned to look at Marylou, to tell her she would split it with her, for the children. Marylou jerked the large fiberboard check from her hands and whacked Joelle over the head with it.

And that was how Joelle won a major prize on a popular game show, and celebrated in the E.R.

## Scene with Character #2:

"We'll start the final round in a few minutes," the emcee, Jack Haney, said. "Is everyone clear on the process?"

Ruby lowered her head and glared at him.

"Process?" she asked. "What process? I thought this was a game show."

"What I mean is-"

"Okay, people, we're on in five, four," the director called out, then he held up his fingers: three, two, one...

He pointed at Haney, who turned to the camera with a wide grin and began his spiel. But Ruby didn't listen. She had "process" stuck in her head. She began to shake. Sweat rolled down her face. She looked out at the studio audience and gasped.

They were all processed! Every one of them, processed until they looked like blocks of meats and cheeses, all staring at her, pointing at her, laughing at her. Would that be her fate? What kind of game show was this?

"All right, Wayne, you spin the wheel," Haney said, He glanced past the first contestant to where Ruby stood, shuddering in her shoes. She pulled her shoulders up as though she were a turtle. Haney's face wavered and began to change. She could see it beginning to process right in front of her!

Wayne bent down and grabbed the wheel. little processing gizmos scrabbled up his suit coat, changing him as they went. Ruby stared, mesmerized. Cheese, he was becoming a block of processed cheese. Would hr be able to stand up again?

'They'll process you.'

"What?" ruby asked. She turned around, looking for the speaker.

"Is something wrong, Ruby?" Jack Haney asked. Ruby looked at him. His processed chicken roll face seemed angry, not concerned. He was in on it! He was the mastermind behind the scheme to get her processed!

'You have to win,Ruby,' the voice said, the voice in her head. She hadn't heard it for a while, not while she had been taking those pills. But she'd run out of them, and she hated the way they made her feel, as though her head was stuffed with cotton wool. So she hadn't gone back to the clinic.

"I'm gonna try," she told her interior friend.

"Try what,Ruby?" Haney asked.

"To win, you idiot!"

The audience laughed, all those processes cheeses and chickens and cows and livers. Ruby glared at them and saw a few processed tomato products scattered here and there.

'Only the one who wins doesn't get processed,' the voice intoned, like a bell ringing in her head.

"They won't do it to me," Ruby told the voice. "I'm gonna win right now!"

She shoved the other woman contestant away from the wheel. They hadn't gotten to her yet, she was still unprocessed.

"Run!" Ruby yelled. "Before they get you, too!"

The woman backed away from Ruby but she stayed on the stage. Ruby saw two stage hands start toward her. Jack Haney backed away, too. Processed people were not very brave. But Ruby was brave. She yanked at the wheel and pulled it off its track. Then she ran to the large board where the questions were listed. She began beating on the brittle surface until cracks appeared.

"I'll win! You won't process me! I'll beat you all!" she shrieked, as the stage hands tackled her and dragged her off the stage. The audience applauded. In the control room, the phone lines lit up with callers pleading to be contestants. And their ratings soared into the stratosphere.

## Scene with Character #3:

"We'll begin the final round in a few minutes," the emcee, Jack Haney, said. "Is everyone clear on the process?"

The other two contestants nodded. Jerry stood still, his mind roving back over the detailed instructions he'd memorized just before the show began. Everything so far had been copacetic. Every rule adhered to, every question timed to perfection. He opened his eyes and nodded at Haney just as the director counted down the seconds.

"And we're back, folks," Haney said, turning his 1,000-watt grin to the camera. "The final round stands before us. It's a close game so far.

Lillian, from Decatur, has $2,000. Edmond here, from Tuscaloosa, has garnered $2,800. And Jerry, our Dallas contingent, has a whopping 3,200." He turned the the contestants. Jerry felt his stomach clench. He would do it, win this round and therefore the entire game. Without one mistake on his part. Not one.

"Okay, Lillian, it's your turn first."

Lillian bent forward, grasped the wheel and gave it a mighty push. Jerry was surprised at her strength. She seemed like such a little slip of a woman. Hard to believe she had 7 kids and a high-powered job at a cable company.

The wheel spun and stopped on a 7. *Not bad,* Jerry thought, though he was sure he would do better. He had to. Edmund took his turn and the wheel stopped at a 3. Jerry almost laughed. Now it was his turn. The wheel handle felt cold to his fingers. He reared back and used all his strength in the push. Around and around the wheel went, slowing as it neared the 9. Jerry's heart thudded. He was going to do it! Win the entire game. The wheel slowed, paused, then lurched past the 9 and stopped on the 7.

"We have a tie, people!" Haney crowed, but Jerry barely heard him. A tie! There couldn't be a tie, now they all had to spin again. And time was running out. He felt frozen in place, as though the world had stopped. What would they do now? He felt the ominous weight of tragedy bear down on him.

"Well, what do you say?" Haney looked out into the audience. "How about we let the little lady go first? After all, she did get her 7 first."

The audience applauded with obvious approval. Jerry glared at them. let her go first? Why? Where did it say that in the rules? What if she won the question? Then he would lose by default and he couldn't lose. He simply couldn't.

"No," he said, his nervous hands restless on his tie, his shirt collar, his lapels, his voice strident with disapproval. "That's not fair. It's not in the rules."

"But we always break a tie by what the audience wants," Haney replied, his smile still wide, innocent looking. But Jerry knew it wasn't, not in the least. He was cheating, using his charm and handsome face to get away with it. Didn't he know that horrible things happen when rules aren't followed?

"Come on, Jerry, be a gentleman and let the lady go first. Or we won't have enough time to finish the round." Haney smiled at him again, but Jerry could see his eyes change, see the concern start to grown. *Too late*, he thought.

"We have to follow the rules," Jerry insisted. He walked out from behind the wheel. "Terrible things happen when rules are broken. The world could end. I know." He stepped to stage right and turned to face his opponents. "I've known ever since Rory died, ever since I broke the rules and he paid for it. I can't let you do it. We have to do it right!"

He pulled out the Ruger he'd tucked into his waistband. The audience gasped. Someone screamed and a dozen or so people started to rise.

"Stop!" Jerry yelled. "The show isn't over. You can't leave, not yet. It's against the rules to leave before the game ends."

The audience subsided into a nervous silence. Haney stepped closer to Jerry.

"It's okay, Jerry, we'll do it the right way. Just be careful with that thing, okay?"

"No." Jerry began to shake. "There's not enough time now. It's ruined, all ruined. Because of you!"

He pointed the gun at Lillian, who cowered behind the wheel.

"You spun the same number I did. It's your fault!" Jerry screamed.

Then the lights went out. A loud boom deafened Jerry and he felt the gun kick in his hand.

**The Characters:**

**Scene #1:** A naive young woman who has little confidence in herself and wishes only to please others

**Scene #2:** A schizophrenic woman off her meds

**Scene #3:** A persnickety accountant who lives in terror of breaking the rules

## Lesson 12: Whose Story Is It Anyway?

Here is one scene rendered from 4 different characters. The scene is in a school, where the alarm bell has rung, and danger stalks the corridors. It's fun to do this when you're writing, to see which character provides the most information and pushes the story forward the best.

### Scene 1: from the classroom teacher's POV

The words stuttered in Dana's throat when the bell rang in the middle of class. Jessie, the class cutup, tossed his pencil in the air and shouted, "Saved by the wanking siren!" The rest of the students laughed, but Dana barely noticed. The clanging bell was not the dismissal ring, nor even the pulse of the fire alarm. This was the evacuation bell, a signal something was very wrong.

"Stay in your seats," she told the class, her head thudding in her chest. "Jamie, sit down and shut up! Now!

Jessie stopped mid-guffaw and stared at her, obviously startled by her abrupt tone and words. She'd probably be called on the carpet for that by his rich parents, Dana knew, but she had no time to worry about that now.

"Everyone! Listen to me. I want you all to sit quietly while I find out what is happening. Be ready to move when I tell you to. Leave everything behind."

Dana looked out into the hall and saw David Tremble, the teacher in the room next door. His room had an intercom with the office. If anyone would know what was happening, he would. She stepped outside and shut the door behind her. No sense upsetting the kids yet.

What's happening, Dave?" she asked.

"I don't know. I tried to call the office, but I got only static. Seems quiet, though. I don't smell smoke or any chemicals."

"Do we just stay put?" Dana asked over the claxoning alarm. her head was beginning to pound. Her worst fear was coming true, being responsible for a classroom full of children during an emergency. She couldn't stop her hands from shaking.

The alarm suddenly fell silent. In the muffled distance, she heard what sounded like a car backfiring, and screams abruptly cut off. She turned to her room, determined to get the children to safety. But she couldn't open the door. The safety locks had engaged, locking the children inside, and her out in the hall with whatever was stalking the school.

## Scene #2: from another teacher's POV

The bell startled everyone in the classroom. Becky spilled ink all over her desk and started to cry. Over the piercing siren I could hear Dana's cutup, Jessie, shout, "Saved by the wanking siren!" The roar of laughter filtering through the wall almost drowned out the throbbing claxon.

Damn, I knew this was bad. I wondered if we'd get locked inside our rooms. That's what the emergency instructions said would happen if the alarm didn't cut off within 2 minutes. Angela will think I stood her up for lunch, I thought, never dreaming this was anything but a mistake. I headed for the intercom and punched the button.

"Hey, Marjorie, what's going on?" I asked. I couldn't keep the grin off my face as I pictured the school secretary fluttering in Victorian panic, lace hanky dangling from sweater sleeve. But nothing answered me other than static. I punched the btoon twice more, with the same result.

"Jed, help Becky clean up that mess," I ordered as I headed for the door. "I'll go see what's going on. Stay calm everyone, I'm sure its just a short in the wiring."

I pulled open the door and ran into Dana in the hallway. Great, just what i needed, the only teacher who didn't know how to make a decision. She was shaking like a leaf, her green eyes the only color in her face.

"What's happening, Dave?" she asked.

The alarm's going off, you twit, I thought, but instead told her about the static on the intercom. Her face blanched even whiter and i stared, fascinated that white could actually go pale.

"Do we just stay put?" she asked, her eyes actually glazing with the effort of trying to remain coherent. Who put this idiot in charge of children? I wondered if perhaps her father had bought her her teaching position, if any of her students actually learned anything from her.

Then the alarm cut off. Good, I thought, tempest in a teapot. I had turned back to my room when I heard the gunshots and screams, like this was a fucking TV show or something. The classroom door locked before I could get it open and duck inside. Damn. Now I was stuck out in the hall with whatever was heading our way. I wondered if I would be in more danger from the bad guys or from lily-livered Dana the teacher.

## Scene #3: from a female student's POV

I shouldn't have been in the hall, but I'd skipped out of Chemistry class three times before and hadn't gotten caught. Why should this time be any different? Old Mr. Jaynes couldn't see as far as the back of the room where I sat, and Debbie always answered "here" for me when he called roll. And I knew the teachers in this wing never wandered around the hallways, so I figured I'd just hunker down in the recessed doorway to the one unoccupied room and finish the poem I'd started last night.

Brandon. I sighed as I picked up my pen. Would he recognize himself in my words, understand how important he was to me? I set the pen on the page and a loud screech burst next to my ear. My pen skittered across the page, leaving a gouge, and clattered onto the tile floor.

I cowered against the wall, hands over my ears, the wailing of the siren stabbing into the pit of my stomach. What the hell was going on? I'd been going to this school for 9 years and I'd never heard this sound before. I stood up to sneak back to Chem class before I got caught, but before I could move, Mr. Tremble stepped out into the hall.

God, he's gorgeous, I thought, wondering why I never lucked out with a teacher like him. I always got the Mr. Magoo look-alikes. He was so aptly named, Mr Tremble - that's what he made my hart do. No one else was around. Maybe I could wander by, all scared and lost-like, and he'd put his arm around me...

Drat. Now Miss Utley's door was opening and out she came. Mr Tremble would never look at me, a lowly ninth-grader, with a beauty queen like "Utterly G," as the boys all called her (g for gorgeous and damn she really was) around. She walked up to him, put her hands on his chest - I shivered inside at what his chest must feel like beneath her hands - and asked him something. Damn alarm was so loud I couldn't hear what.

Mr. Tremble gave her an annoyed look, then answered her back. He took a step away from her and glanced down the hall toward me. But I don't think he saw me, he just stared at the door to the west wing. Then Utterly G asked him something else and the alarm stopped.

I couldn't believe how loud the silence was! I watched Mr Tremble yank on his classroom door. It wouldn't open, nor would Utterly G's. It wasn't until I saw the panic cross their faces that I realized the muted sounds I was hearing were screams and gunshots. Did Danny bring his Dad's gun to shoot the PT teacher like he said he was going to do? Somehow I didn't think I'd get into trouble for cutting Chem class any more.

## Scene #4: from a male student's POV

Jessie couldn't believe it when the siren went off. Just before the surprise test! Hooray! How lucky could a guy get?

"Saved by the wanking siren!" he shouted and tossed his pencil in the air.

All the kids laughed, which usually got Utterly G's goat. But instead of yelling at everyone, she dithered around in a circle and then began barking orders.

"Jessie, sit down and shut up!" She was trying to be firm, but even Jessie could hear the wobble in her voice. She was scared. Of a siren. Jessie couldn't believe it.

And she was stupid, too. Teach might be a looker but here she was telling him to shut up instead of screeching about his profanity. Obviously, she didn't spend much time on BBC America. Jessie couldn't stop the grin that broke out across his face.

As soon as the door shut behind her, Jessie was up like a shot.

"Chris, man the door!" he ordered, and pansy-ass Chris leapt to obey. "What is she doing?"

Jessie headed for Utterly G's desk and the dreaded test while Chris peered through the glass panel. He shuffled among the papers, searching for the answer key.

"She's talking to Mr. Tremble," Chris said, his own voice trembling. Mr T was tough, always kept the boys in line. Not even Jessie wanted to tangle with him.

"Keep your eyes peeled. Let me know if they're heading this way." Jessie snatched up the answer sheet and turned to the rest of the class. "Okay, take out your cheat sheets," he called over the noise of the siren. "Number one is A, two is C, three -"

The siren cut off. Silence descended. Well, that will make it easier, if she'll just stay out there a little longer, Jessie thought. Then he heard what sounded like muffled gunshots and screams. His heart stuttered in his chest. Kurt had vowed to get Jessie for beating up his little brother last week. Could it be him, shooting his way toward Utterly G's classroom? Jessie looked over at the door, saw Teach's ashen face looking in the window, her expression one of pure panic. The answer key dropped from his suddenly numb fingers. He looked around, found nowhere to hide. Maybe he wasn't so lucky after all.

## Lesson #15: POV Inconsistencies

For each of the examples, I have underlined the inconsistency and noted what it is and what needs to be done to correct it.

**Example #1:** From author Laurie Woodward: www.artania.com

I walked in the shadow of the neon forest for hours, eyes blinking in bewilderment. Recognizing nothing. Not a single street or building was familiar. How long had I been watching the trash shuffle beneath my feet? Where had this journey begun? Did it even have a beginning?

Off in the distance I heard someone humming and surprised myself by joining in. I was somehow drawn to the ephemeral music. My shadow bounced ahead of me as I moved toward the sound. Beneath the yellow spotlight of a used car lot a second shadow joined my own.

I drew closer to the figure and slowed. Wire-rimmed spectacles reflected a fugue of light that momentarily blinded me. I faltered and would have fallen had it not been for the outstretched arms of my spot lit partner.

"Aye bloke. Stumbling again, are we?" asked the Stranger. <u>He had waited long for the Lost One's return and felt neon bubbles coursing through each vein at his touch.</u>

"I couldn't see." I replied. "Your glasses. They were so bright. A kaleidoscope of color."

(How can the "I" know that the stranger had waited long and what he felt at each touch? Solution: either delete this entire sentence, or have the stranger tell the speaker he had been waiting, then let him react when the speaker touches him and have the speaker surmise why he reacted that way.)

**Example #2:** From Sue McGinty's new Bella Kowalski mystery, "Murder in Mariposa Bay." www.suemcginty.com (written wrong for this specific

Pisniak tears the application for campground handyman in two, deposits it in the recycle bin and grinds his cigarette into the dirt with the toe of his boot. He lowers the cap over his eyes, then thinks better of it and hides it in the trash beneath a paper bag. Goodbye old friend. Head down, eyes averted, he hurries to his pickup.

<u>Because his eyes are focused elsewhere, the man once known as Steve Pisniak doesn't see his former friend peer over the top of his newspaper, doesn't notice the Escalade parked near the restroom, doesn't observe the old geezer behind the wheel put a cell phone to his ear, doesn't hear the call that will end his life.</u>

(This is an example of a disinterested narrator who hovers above the action and tells what the POV character cannot see, hear or know. It is Classic Omniscience and doesn't belong in an Emotional Omniscient POV piece. Either delete the entire paragraph, or do a line break and go into the former friend's POV to relay this information.)

**Example #3:** From author Mark Arnold (markarnoldphd@gmail.com)

"Please Kyle!" *I have to hear it*, she thought, fighting to catch her breath. "Please!"

Kyle drew back. "What?"

"I have to know. Do you love me?" She sounded like a hungry kitten.

Every time in every relationship there is that moment, the one when they wanted more than a gesture, more than dedication, more than commitment. There was the moment you had to say, The Word.

"You know I do." More kisses, and more, and . . .

"Please Kyle!" Again, <u>I voiced the breathless request</u> as old as time. "Say it!"

Kyle tried to focus inside the faintly musty scent of back-seat fabric, the pounding rain on the roof of the car, the slickness of the steamy windows where bare hands and feet fighting for purchase slid and squeaked.

"Oh, baby, listen with your heart." *Sincerity. Yeah that's it.*

(This passage is written in Shifting Thirds POV, except for the underlined part, which slips into First Person POV. Change the 'I' to 'she' to fix it. To take it out of Shifting Thirds, simply use either the man or the woman as the POV character and delete all inner thoughts, emotions and assumptions by the other character.)

**Example #4:** From Tony Piazza (www.authortonypiazza.com)

Paris is the city of romance, or so they say. Not for this journalist. On this occasion I was sitting at a sidewalk café watching a couple across the aisle whispering sweet endearments to each other. Depressed I sipped on my espresso gazing sullenly up at the gray sky and then down towards the featureless crowds that passed before me. Loneliness had now reached my soul, an emptiness as barren as the trees which lined the boulevard along the Seine, and as hollow as the taps of gentle rain hitting the awning above me.

"Is this seat taken?" A woman suddenly asked, her request taking me by surprise.

"Please," I offered. My first glance saw that she was charming, and she likewise studied my face and <u>thought that she had finally found the kind of man she'd been searching for</u>.

(How can the POV character know what is in the woman's mind? He can only see that she is studying him. Anything else is a conjecture on his part. To fix it, you could write: "...studied my face as though she had finally found..." That puts it in the man's perspective because it's his assumption. For all he knows, she could be disappointed in him, or looking for a flaw, or wondering how to kill him.)

**Example #5:** From Tony Piazza (www.authortonypiazza.com)

The old man slipped off the burro and wandered aimlessly towards the mounds of sand that filled his horizon. He stumbled a few times on his way, but always seemed to pick himself up—an outward sign of his firm determination. <u>I may have been delirious from the heat, or just driven mad by my lust for the gold, but for whatever reason I just kept moving ahead even if I hadn't any real destination in mind</u>.

(Again, a slip from Third Person POV to First Person POV. To fix this, put the underlined portion into Third Person, or put the non-underlined portion into First Person.)

**Example #6:** From Susan Tuttle's soon-to-be-released mystery, "Piece By Piece," (www.SusanTuttleWrites.com)

The phone rang, shattering the early morning silence. Ogden Wilkes glanced at the clock as he snatched up the receiver. 4:10 am. He knew it had to be more than important. Only the wounding of one of his men was serious enough to drag the precinct captain out of his comfortable bed.

He held the phone to his chest a moment, waiting until his heart slowed and his mind began working again. The events of the last thirty-six hours filtered through his consciousness and he was amazed that he'd actually fallen asleep. His wife, Judy, <u>awakened by the ring</u>, muttered an incoherent sound and turned over, put her back to him. Wilkes inched his way to the padded headboard and brought the receiver to his ear.

"Yes, what is it?" His quiet voice seemed to echo in the still room.

His dog, Musuko, asleep on the floor under the partially open window, sat up, head cocked, ears alert, paws restless on the carpet, <u>eager to share in the nighttime excitement</u>.

"Traynor here, Captain. I'm with Selling, in an alley down by the river, between Fourth and Lexington. I think you'd better get down here."

"Who is it?" Wilkes threw back the covers and swung his feet to the floor.

"Cliff Davisson."

(There are two POV problems in this passage. First, how can Wilkes know that the phone awakened his wife? It might be a logical conclusion, but she might not have been asleep anyway. Fix it by either eliminating it, or adding a disclaimer that puts in in Wilkes' perspective:

obviously awakened, or probably awakened [I would leave it out mainly because it's not relevant information that the phone awakened his wife]. The second switch goes into the **dog's** POV. Wilkes cannot know, though he can surmise, that the dog is eager to share the excitement of his master awake at night. He could just need to go outside. Or he could have heard a raccoon on the roof. Again, fix it with a disclaimer like 'obviously eager,' or 'appearing eager,' or eliminate it altogether since the cocked head, alert ears and restless paws already show the dog is excited and eager.)

# Afterword

*"All readers come to fiction as willing accomplices to your lies. Such is the basic goodwill contract made the moment we pick up a work of fiction."*

~Steve Almond, WD

**POINT OF VIEW IS** a journey, one that doesn't end with a few exercises but continues to travel deeper and deeper into the hearts and minds of your story's characters. It's a way of looking at the world and the people in it with eyes that see more than what most people see, and a mind that can sort what the eyes see into meaningful stories that entertain, amuse, edify and instruct the reader.

But while Point of View is one of the most important concepts you need to understand to write compelling, fascinating stories, it is only one of the twelve essential fiction writing skills you need to master. Among them are creating characters, crafting settings, discovering interesting story ideas, developing a unique voice, writing effective scenes, crafting compelling plots, creating realistic dialogue, interweaving fascinating subplots, etc.

So, where do you go from here? How do you master the twelve major skills needed to unlock the stories that reside deep within your psyche?

***Write It Right: Exercises to Unlock the Writer in Everyone*** can show you how.

***Workbook #1*** consists of the first three units of the ***Write It Right*** series: ***Character, Setting*** and ***Story.*** These are the first three essential elements of story telling, the foundation blocks, so to speak, for without compelling characters in unforgettable settings acting out amazing stories, there is nothing to write about. Unit #1, *Character*, gives you 9 lessons to help you create amazing characters readers will want to know about. The second unit, *Setting*, consists of 7 lessons and exercises on crafting compelling settings that will draw readers into your story world. And the third unit, *Story*, presents 10 lessons on how to find and assess story ideas that readers will clamor for.

***Workbook #3: Plot, Dialogue*** continues your journey along the writer's path with the fifth unit, *Plot*, and its 8 exercises on crafting flawless, intricate plots that sizzle off the page. You'll discover what plot actually is, the importance of a through line, how to analyze ideas for viable plots and where to find plots in the world around you. The sixth unit, *Dialogue*, presents 8 lessons that will show you how to write sparkling dialogue that sounds perfectly natural while still addressing the six necessary ingredients that make dialogue an integral part of the story. You will learn how to write for your audience, make your characters' voices unique, use idioms to infuse verisimilitude, how to tag properly and how to incorporate subtext into what your characters say.

***Workbook #4: Scenes, Style/Voice*** contains the seventh unit, *Scenes*, which gives you 11 lessons and exercises that will help you understand the 9 different types of scene structures and how they affect the rhythm and pacing of your stories, as well as the Scene Question and transitioning between scenes. The eighth unit, *Style/Voice*, offers 9 lessons to help you understand the unique way you see and interpret the world, which will help you develop a clear, consistent voice and style that will stand out among all the others and be readily recognizable as yours alone.

***Workbook #5: Conflict/Tension, Subplot*** presents 9 lessons in the ninth unit, *Conflict/Tension*, that will show you how to create and sustain the tension that keeps readers turning pages through a series of 9 tension-filled exercises. The strategies contained in the tenth unit, *Subplot*, will help you add depth and dimension to your work by weaving fascinating subplots into your main stories. In this workbook, you will also learn the secret to creating an effective and compelling series that satisfies readers as it pulls them through one volume to the next.

***Workbook #6: Beginnings, Endings*** gives you 8 different formats each for opening your story and for ending your story. In the eleventh unit, *Brilliant Beginnings*, you will also learn how to polish that all-important first sentence/first paragraph/first page so that readers are compelled to continue reading. And in the twelfth unit, *Extraordinary Endings*, you will learn the secrets to choosing the proper ending for whatever story you write, so that readers smile and say, "I'm so glad I read that!"

Look for the entire *Write It Right: Exercises to Unlock the Writer in Everyone* workbook series on Amazon.com in print format. Each individual unit will also eventually be available in digital format in the Kindle store, but the workbooks themselves are available only in print because I feel that is the most useful format for serious writers. You can have the book open on your desk as you work on the exercises either by hand or on the computer, and not have to keep switching from one window to another to check on the exercise parameters or re-read the lesson as you work.

Thank you for purchasing this Workbook. I hope you find it helpful on your writing journey. If you do, please take the time to write a review on Amazon.com, since that's where most of my sales come from. In this digital age of social media, it's reader reviews that best help sell books. As does word of mouth, so be sure to tell all your writer friends about the *Write It Right* series, so they can also benefit from the program.

Also, if you'd like, please drop by my website (www.SusanTuttleWrites.com) and leave a comment or two about the photos and story/character/setting ideas you'll find (Category: Woman of 1,000 Words), the weekly writing prompts that post every Wednesday (Category: Write Over The Hump), about the *Write It Right* program, or any other writing subject that comes to mind. Or email me at aim2write@yahoo.com. I'd love to hear from you.

# Susan's Books

*I NEVER THOUGHT, WHEN* I started to write my own stories, that one day I would produce an entire series of workbooks on how to write fiction (and creative nonfiction, because these days that genre needs to be structured in the same manner as fiction). I never thought it even when I started teaching fiction writing. Getting my novels out was my main goal. But life has a way of guiding you down paths you don't even know are there, and this is where I've been led.

What follows is a listing of the books I have out in either print or ebook format, or both—and those in process of being readied for print/e-format. The **Write It Right Workbooks** head the list, but I'm also adding in my fiction titles at the end (suspense and paranormal suspense) in case you might like to take a peek at them, too (all available on Amazon.com and Amazon Kindle). I think they're pretty great, but then, as the author, I'll admit I'm a bit prejudiced.

My hope is that my **Write It Right Workbooks** will help unlock the talent and amazing stories that reside in each and every one of you. Happy writing!

# Susan's Nonfiction Books

**Write It Right Workbooks available from Amazon Print:**
Workbook #1: Units 1, 2, 3: Character, Setting, Story
Workbook #2: Unit 4: POV,
Workbook #3: Units 5, 6: Plot, Dialogue
Workbook #4: Units 7, 8: Scenes, Style/Voice, Conflict
Workbook #5: Units 9, 10: Conflict/Tension, Subplot*
Workbook #6: Units 11, 12: Beginnings, Endings*

**Write It Right Individual Units available from Amazon Kindle:**
Volume 1: Character
Volume 2: Setting
Volume 3: Story
Volume 4: Point of View (POV)
Volume 5: Plot*
Volume 6: Dialogue*
Volume 7: Scenes*
Volume 8: Style and Voice*
Volume 9: Conflict/Tension*
Volume 10: Subplot*
Volume 11: Brilliant Beginnings*
Volume 12: Extraordinary Endings*

*Coming Soon

# Susan's Fiction Books

**Suspense**
*Tangled Webs*
*Sins of the Past*

**Paranormal Suspense**
*Proof of Identity*

Coming Soon:
*Piece By Piece,* suspense
*Obsession,* suspense
*A Matter of Identity,* historical suspense
*Stealing Shyon,* an adult fantasy
The Skylark Series: paranormal detectives
   *The Somewhen Murder*
   *Dead Ringer*
   *Someone Else's Eyes*
   *Tattoed in Death*
*Destany's Daughter,* Volume 1 of a paranormal YA/Adult fantasy quadrilogy
*It Takes Class: On The Short Side,* free writes from my classes

www.ingramcontent.com/pod-product-compliance
Lightning Source LLC
Chambersburg PA
CBHW081355040426
42451CB00017B/3454